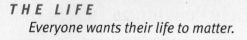

THE LIFE
Everyone wants their life to matter.

The Life: What's Inside

What Does It Mean to "Remain" in Jesus? 50

Ordinary People Given God's Power 69 Acts 2:1-47

The Choice 103

Editor-in-Chief: Dave Rahn

Editor: Keith Williams

Designer: Dan Farrell

Consulting Editors: Nina Edwards,
Ebonie Davis, Kara Pritchard,
Mark Larson, Kate Huff, Kelsey
Bushnell, Kevin Becht

Visit Tyndale online at www.newlivingtranslation.com and www.tyndale.com.
Visit Youth for Christ online at www.yfc.net.

The Life is an edition of the Holy Bible, New Living Translation. *Holy Bible*, New
Living Translation copyright © 1996, 2004, 2007, 2013 by Tyndale House
Foundation. All rights reserved.

Features and helps copyright © 2014 by Youth For Christ.

TYNDALE, New Living Translation, NLT, the New Living Translation logo, and
Tyndale's quill logo are registered trademarks of Tyndale House Publishers, Inc.
Youth for Christ and the Youth for Christ logo are registered trademarks of Youth
for Christ/USA, Inc.

Cover photograph used courtesy of Charlie Foster/Unsplash.com.
Back cover photograph courtesy of Guillaume/Unsplash.com.

ISBN 978-1-4143-9636-1 Softcover
Printed in China

Welcome to The Life.

In these pages you can begin to get acquainted with God's story through reading the story of the life of Jesus and his earliest followers straight from the Bible—or at least part of the Bible (there's plenty more where this came from).

But you might be surprised to find that this is not just God's story: It is actually about your story, too. Up to this point you might have thought God's story doesn't have much to do with your story—or anybody else's, for that matter.

Think about everyone's story as a circle. Maybe you would draw the relationship between your story and God's story like this...

But that's not really right, is it? Our stories are all connected. At the very least the Bible shows us that God's story touches us all. Even when we don't see how.

This is better...

Drawing circles that represent life stories can also help us think about whose stories overlap the most with our own.

For example, you might think differently about your friend and your best friend.

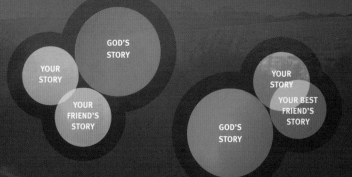

When we read the Bible with open minds, we'll notice that God is trying to help us know enough about his story so that we can join with him, letting him shape our own stories and those of others.

What would it look like for more and more of your life story to be intertwined with more and more of God's?

As you'll read here, Jesus Christ came to show us how that works. *Jesus is the centerpiece of God's story.*

That's why we chose these portions of the Bible. No matter how you might draw your connection with God right now, in these pages you can learn about God for yourself through the writings of those who knew Jesus Christ personally.

And your connection with God can change.

For the moment, set aside others' stories (their story) and imagine how your story could be different if you get totally caught up in God's story. What's stopping you? Start reading!

GOD'S STORY

YOUR STORY

THEIR STORY

THE BOOK OF JOHN

The Bible gives us four Gospels—books that tell the story of who Jesus is and why it matters. John was written by one of his closest followers, an eyewitness to Jesus' life and teachings.

Jesus Is No Ordinary Man

CHAPTER 1

¹:¹In the beginning the Word already existed.
The Word was with God,
and the Word was God.
² He existed in the beginning with God.
³ God created everything through him,
and nothing was created except through him.
⁴ The Word gave life to everything that was created,
and his life brought light to everyone.
⁵ The light shines in the darkness,
and the darkness can never extinguish it.

⁶God sent a man, John the Baptist, ⁷to tell about the light so that everyone might believe because of his testimony. ⁸John himself was not the light; he was simply a witness to tell about the light. ⁹The one who is the true light, who gives light to everyone, was coming into the world.

¹⁰He came into the very world he created, but the world didn't recognize him. ¹¹He came to his own people, and even they rejected him. ¹²But to all who believed him and accepted him, he gave the right to become children of God. ¹³They are reborn—not with a physical birth resulting from human passion or plan, but a birth that comes from God.

¹⁴So the Word became human and made his home among us. He was full of unfailing love and faithfulness. And we have seen his glory, the glory of the Father's one and only Son.

¹⁵John testified about him when he shouted to the crowds, "This is the one I was talking about when I said, 'Someone is coming after me who is far greater than I am, for he existed long before me.'"

¹⁶From his abundance we have all

Jesus is God. He was there from the beginning of everything. In fact, everything was created through him.

> **Jesus is a willing and perfect sacrifice who deals with our sin problem—our self-centered DNA that keeps us from God.**

received one gracious blessing after another. [17] For the law was given through Moses, but God's unfailing love and faithfulness came through Jesus Christ. [18] No one has ever seen God. But the unique One, who is himself God, is near to the Father's heart. He has revealed God to us.

John the Baptist Identifies Himself

[19] This was John's testimony when the Jewish leaders sent priests and Temple assistants from Jerusalem to ask John, "Who are you?" [20] He came right out and said, "I am not the Messiah."

[21] "Well then, who are you?" they asked. "Are you Elijah?"

"No," he replied.

"Are you the Prophet we are expecting?"

"No."

[22] "Then who are you? We need an answer for those who sent us. What do you have to say about yourself?"

[23] John replied in the words of the prophet Isaiah:

"I am a voice shouting in the wilderness,
'Clear the way for the LORD's coming!'"

[24] Then the Pharisees who had been sent [25] asked him, "If you aren't the Messiah or Elijah or the Prophet, what right do you have to baptize?"

[26] John told them, "I baptize with water, but right here in the crowd is someone you do not recognize. [27] Though his ministry follows mine, I'm not even worthy to be his slave and untie the straps of his sandal."

[28] This encounter took place in Bethany, an area east of the Jordan River, where John was baptizing.

Jesus Is Greater than John

[29] The next day John saw Jesus coming toward him and said, "Look! The Lamb of God who takes away the sin of the world! [30] He is the one I was talking about when I said, 'A man is coming after me who is far greater than I am, for he existed long before

me.' ³¹I did not recognize him as the Messiah, but I have been baptizing with water so that he might be revealed to Israel."

³²Then John testified, "I saw the Holy Spirit descending like a dove from heaven and resting upon him. ³³I didn't know he was the one, but when God sent me to baptize with water, he told me, 'The one on whom you see the Spirit descend and rest is the one who will baptize with the Holy Spirit.' ³⁴I saw this happen to Jesus, so I testify that he is the Chosen One of God."

Jesus' First Followers

³⁵The following day John was again standing with two of his disciples. ³⁶As Jesus walked by, John looked at him and declared, "Look! There is the Lamb of God!" ³⁷When John's two disciples heard this, they followed Jesus.

³⁸Jesus looked around and saw them following. "What do you want?" he asked them.

They replied, "Rabbi" (which means "Teacher"), "where are you staying?"

³⁹"Come and see," he said. It was about four o'clock in the afternoon when they went with him to the place where he was staying, and they remained with him the rest of the day.

⁴⁰Andrew, Simon Peter's brother, was one of these men who heard what John said and then followed Jesus. ⁴¹Andrew went to find his brother, Simon, and told him, "We have found the Messiah" (which means "Christ").

⁴²Then Andrew brought Simon to meet Jesus. Looking intently at Simon, Jesus said, "Your name is Simon, son of John—but you will be called Cephas" (which means "Peter").

⁴³The next day Jesus decided to go to Galilee. He found Philip and said to him, "Come, follow me." ⁴⁴Philip was from Bethsaida, Andrew and Peter's hometown.

⁴⁵Philip went to look for Nathanael and told him, "We have found the very person Moses and the prophets wrote about! His name is Jesus, the son of Joseph from Nazareth."

⁴⁶"Nazareth!" exclaimed Nathanael. "Can anything good come from Nazareth?"

"Come and see for yourself," Philip replied.

⁴⁷As they approached, Jesus said, "Now here is a genuine son of Israel—a man of complete integrity."

⁴⁸"How do you know about me?" Nathanael asked.

Jesus replied, "I could see you under the fig tree before Philip found you."

⁴⁹Then Nathanael exclaimed, "Rabbi, you are the Son of God—the King of Israel!"

⁵⁰Jesus asked him, "Do you believe this just because I told you I had seen you under the fig tree? You will see greater things than this." ⁵¹Then he said, "I tell you the truth, you will all see heaven open and the angels of God going up and down on the Son of Man, the one who is the stairway between heaven and earth."

Jesus Makes His Presence Known

2:¹The next day there was a wedding celebration in the village of Cana in Galilee. Jesus' mother was there, ²and

Jesus Attracts People From the Margins

O NE DAY AS JESUS WAS PREACHING on the shore of the Sea of Galilee, great crowds pressed in on him to listen to the word of God. [2]He noticed two empty boats at the water's edge, for the fishermen had left them and were washing their nets. [3]Stepping into one of the boats, Jesus asked Simon, its owner, to push it out into the water. So he sat in the boat and taught the crowds from there.

[4]When he had finished speaking, he said to Simon, "Now go out where it is deeper, and let down your nets to catch some fish."

[5]"Master," Simon replied, "we worked hard all last night and didn't catch a thing. But if you say so, I'll let the nets down again." [6]And this time their nets were so full of fish they began to tear! [7]A shout for help brought their partners in the other boat, and soon both boats were filled with fish and on the verge of sinking.

When Simon Peter realized what had happened, he fell to his knees before Jesus and said, "Oh, Lord, please leave me—I'm too much of a sinner to be around you." For he was awestruck by the number of fish they had caught, as were the others with him. His partners, James and John, the sons of Zebedee, were also amazed.

Jesus replied to Simon, "Don't be afraid! From now on you'll be fishing for people!" And as soon as they landed, they left everything and followed Jesus.

Jesus Heals a Man with Leprosy

[12]In one of the villages, Jesus met a man with an advanced case of leprosy. When the man saw Jesus, he bowed with his face to the ground, begging to be healed. "Lord," he said, "if you are willing, you can heal me and make me clean."

[13]Jesus reached out and touched him. "I am willing," he said. "Be healed!" And instantly the leprosy disappeared. [14]Then Jesus

Jesus is popular, but not like a movie star. He's more like the guy everybody wants to be around because he is both kind and intriguing.

instructed him not to tell anyone what had happened. He said, "Go to the priest and let him examine you. Take along the offering required in the law of Moses for those who have been healed of leprosy. This will be a public testimony that you have been cleansed."

[15]But despite Jesus' instructions, the report of his power spread even faster, and vast crowds came to hear him preach and to be healed of their diseases. [16] But Jesus often withdrew to the wilderness for prayer.

Jesus Heals a Paralyzed Man

[17]One day while Jesus was teaching, some Pharisees and teachers of religious law were sitting nearby. (It seemed that these men showed up from every village in all Galilee and Judea, as well as from Jerusalem.) And the Lord's healing power was strongly with Jesus.

¹⁸Some men came carrying a paralyzed man on a sleeping mat. They tried to take him inside to Jesus, ¹⁹but they couldn't reach him because of the crowd. So they went up to the roof and took off some tiles. Then they lowered the sick man on his mat down into the crowd, right in front of Jesus. ²⁰Seeing their faith, Jesus said to the man, "Young man, your sins are forgiven."

²¹But the Pharisees and teachers of religious law said to themselves, "Who does he think he is? That's blasphemy! Only God can forgive sins!"

²²Jesus knew what they were thinking, so he asked them, "Why do you question this in your hearts? ²³Is it easier to say 'Your sins are forgiven,' or 'Stand up and walk'? ²⁴So I will prove to you that the Son of Man has the authority on earth to forgive sins." Then Jesus turned to the paralyzed man and said, "Stand up, pick up your mat, and go home!"

²⁵And immediately, as everyone watched, the man jumped up, picked up his mat, and went home praising God. ²⁶Everyone was gripped with great wonder and awe, and they praised God, exclaiming, "We have seen amazing things today!"

Jesus Accepts Anyone Who Is Willing to Follow Him

²⁷Later, as Jesus left the town, he saw a tax collector named Levi sitting at his tax collector's booth. "Follow me and be my disciple," Jesus said to him. ²⁸So Levi got up, left everything, and followed him.

²⁹Later, Levi held a banquet in his home with Jesus as the guest of honor. Many of Levi's fellow tax collectors and other guests also ate with them. ³⁰But the Pharisees and their teachers of religious law complained bitterly to Jesus' disciples, "Why do you eat and drink with such scum?"

³¹Jesus answered them, "Healthy people don't need a doctor—sick people do. ³²I have come to call not those who think they are righteous, but those who know they are sinners and need to repent." ∎

/// *continued from page 3*

Jesus and his disciples were also invited to the celebration. ³The wine supply ran out during the festivities, so Jesus' mother told him, "They have no more wine."

⁴"Dear woman, that's not our problem," Jesus replied. "My time has not yet come."

⁵But his mother told the servants, "Do whatever he tells you."

⁶Standing nearby were six stone water jars, used for Jewish ceremonial washing. Each could hold twenty to thirty gallons. ⁷Jesus told the servants, "Fill the jars with water." When the jars had been filled, ⁸he said, "Now dip some out, and take it to the master of ceremonies." So the servants followed his instructions.

⁹When the master of ceremonies tasted the water that was now wine, not knowing where it had come from (though, of course, the servants knew), he called the bridegroom over. ¹⁰"A host always serves the best wine first," he said. "Then, when everyone has had a lot to drink, he brings out the less expensive wine. But you have kept the best until now!"

¹¹This miraculous sign at Cana in Galilee was the first time Jesus revealed his glory. And his disciples believed in him.

¹²After the wedding he went to Capernaum for a few days with his mother, his brothers, and his disciples.

Jesus Rages against Hypocrisy

¹³It was nearly time for the Jewish Passover celebration, so Jesus went to Jerusalem. ¹⁴In the Temple area he saw merchants selling cattle, sheep, and

Jesus is more likely to be the life of the party than you probably imagine.

doves for sacrifices; he also saw dealers at tables exchanging foreign money. ¹⁵Jesus made a whip from some ropes and chased them all out of the Temple. He drove out the sheep and cattle, scattered the money changers' coins over the floor, and turned over their tables. ¹⁶Then, going over to the people who sold doves, he told them, "Get these things out of here. Stop turning my Father's house into a marketplace!"

¹⁷Then his disciples remembered this prophecy from the Scriptures: "Passion for God's house will consume me."

¹⁸But the Jewish leaders demanded,

"What are you doing? If God gave you authority to do this, show us a miraculous sign to prove it."

[19] "All right," Jesus replied. "Destroy this temple, and in three days I will raise it up."

[20] "What!" they exclaimed. "It has taken forty-six years to build this Temple, and you can rebuild it in three days?" [21] But when Jesus said "this temple," he meant his own body. [22] After he was raised from the dead, his disciples remembered he had said this, and they believed both the Scriptures and what Jesus had said.

Surprising Encounters with Jesus

[23] Because of the miraculous signs Jesus did in Jerusalem at the Passover celebration, many began to trust in him. [24] But Jesus didn't trust them, because he knew all about people. [25] No one needed to tell him about human nature, for he knew what was in each person's heart.

[3:1] There was a man named Nicodemus, a Jewish religious leader who was a Pharisee. [2] After dark one evening, he came to speak with Jesus. "Rabbi," he said, "we all know that God has sent you to teach us. Your miraculous signs are evidence that God is with you."

[3] Jesus replied, "I tell you the truth, unless you are born again, you cannot see the Kingdom of God."

[4] "What do you mean?" exclaimed Nicodemus. "How can an old man go back into his mother's womb and be born again?"

[5] Jesus replied, "I assure you, no one can enter the Kingdom of God without being born of water and the Spirit. [6] Humans can reproduce only human life, but the Holy Spirit gives birth to spiritual life. [7] So don't be surprised when I say, 'You must be born again.' [8] The wind blows wherever it wants. Just as you can hear the wind but can't tell where it comes from or where it is going, so you can't explain how people are born of the Spirit."

[9] "How are these things possible?" Nicodemus asked.

[10] Jesus replied, "You are a respected Jewish teacher, and yet you don't understand these things? [11] I assure you, we tell you what we know and have seen, and yet you won't believe our testimony. [12] But if you don't believe me when I tell you about earthly things, how can you possibly believe if I tell you about heavenly things? [13] No one has ever gone to heaven and returned. But the Son of Man has come down from heaven. [14] And as Moses lifted up the bronze snake on a pole in the wilderness, so the Son of Man must be lifted up, [15] so that everyone who believes in him will have eternal life.

[16] "For this is how God loved the world: He gave his one and only Son, so that everyone who believes in him will not perish but have eternal life. [17] God sent his Son into the world not to judge the world, but to save the world through him.

[18] "There is no judgment against anyone who believes in him. But anyone who does not believe in him has already been judged for not believing

in God's one and only Son. [19]And the judgment is based on this fact: God's light came into the world, but people loved the darkness more than the light, for their actions were evil. [20]All who do evil hate the light and refuse to go near it for fear their sins will be exposed. [21]But those who do what is right come to the light so others can see that they are doing what God wants."

He Must Become Greater, I Must Become Less

[22]Then Jesus and his disciples left Jerusalem and went into the Judean countryside. Jesus spent some time with them there, baptizing people.

Messiah. I am only here to prepare the way for him.' [29]It is the bridegroom who marries the bride, and the best man is simply glad to stand with him and hear his vows. Therefore, I am filled with joy at his success. [30]He must become greater and greater, and I must become less and less.

[31]"He has come from above and is greater than anyone else. We are of the earth, and we speak of earthly things, but he has come from heaven and is greater than anyone else. [32]He testifies about what he has seen and heard, but how few believe what he tells them! [33]Anyone who accepts his testimony

Jesus says there's a whole other dimension to life for those who experience a new (spiritual) birth. Are you ready to trust Jesus on this subject?

[23]At this time John the Baptist was baptizing at Aenon, near Salim, because there was plenty of water there; and people kept coming to him for baptism. [24](This was before John was thrown into prison.) [25]A debate broke out between John's disciples and a certain Jew over ceremonial cleansing. [26]So John's disciples came to him and said, "Rabbi, the man you met on the other side of the Jordan River, the one you identified as the Messiah, is also baptizing people. And everybody is going to him instead of coming to us."

[27]John replied, "No one can receive anything unless God gives it from heaven. [28]You yourselves know how plainly I told you, 'I am not the

can affirm that God is true. [34]For he is sent by God. He speaks God's words, for God gives him the Spirit without limit. [35]The Father loves his Son and has put everything into his hands. [36]And anyone who believes in God's Son has eternal life. Anyone who doesn't obey the Son will never experience eternal life but remains under God's angry judgment."

Jesus Talks With the Wrong Kind of Woman

[4:1]Jesus knew the Pharisees had heard that he was baptizing and making more disciples than John [2](though Jesus himself didn't baptize them—his disciples did). ³So he left Judea and returned to Galilee.

⁴He had to go through Samaria on the way. ⁵Eventually he came to the Samaritan village of Sychar, near the field that Jacob gave to his son Joseph.

think you're greater than our ancestor Jacob, who gave us this well? How can you offer better water than he and his sons and his animals enjoyed?"

¹³Jesus replied, "Anyone who drinks this water will soon become thirsty

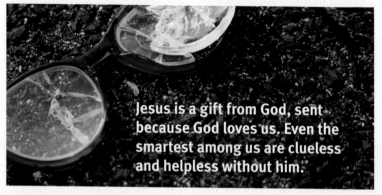

Jesus is a gift from God, sent because God loves us. Even the smartest among us are clueless and helpless without him.

© CHRISTOPHER PATTBERG/PHOTOS.COM

⁶Jacob's well was there; and Jesus, tired from the long walk, sat wearily beside the well about noontime. ⁷Soon a Samaritan woman came to draw water, and Jesus said to her, "Please give me a drink." ⁸He was alone at the time because his disciples had gone into the village to buy some food.

⁹The woman was surprised, for Jews refuse to have anything to do with Samaritans. She said to Jesus, "You are a Jew, and I am a Samaritan woman. Why are you asking me for a drink?"

¹⁰Jesus replied, "If you only knew the gift God has for you and who you are speaking to, you would ask me, and I would give you living water."

¹¹"But sir, you don't have a rope or a bucket," she said, "and this well is very deep. Where would you get this living water? ¹²And besides, do you

again. ¹⁴But those who drink the water I give will never be thirsty again. It becomes a fresh, bubbling spring within them, giving them eternal life."

¹⁵"Please, sir," the woman said, "give me this water! Then I'll never be thirsty again, and I won't have to come here to get water."

¹⁶"Go and get your husband," Jesus told her.

¹⁷"I don't have a husband," the woman replied.

Jesus said, "You're right! You don't have a husband—¹⁸for you have had five husbands, and you aren't even married to the man you're living with now. You certainly spoke the truth!"

¹⁹"Sir," the woman said, "you must be a prophet. ²⁰So tell me, why is it that you Jews insist that Jerusalem is the only place of worship, while

we Samaritans claim it is here at Mount Gerizim, where our ancestors worshiped?"

²¹Jesus replied, "Believe me, dear woman, the time is coming when it will no longer matter whether you worship the Father on this mountain or in Jerusalem. ²²You Samaritans know very little about the one you worship, while we Jews know all about him, for salvation comes through the Jews. ²³But the time is coming—indeed it's here now—when true worshipers will worship the Father in spirit and in truth. The Father is looking for those who will worship him that way. ²⁴For God is Spirit, so those who worship him must worship in spirit and in truth."

²⁵The woman said, "I know the Messiah is coming—the one who is called Christ. When he comes, he will explain everything to us."

²⁶Then Jesus told her, "I AM the Messiah!"

²⁷Just then his disciples came back. They were shocked to find him talking to a woman, but none of them had the nerve to ask, "What do you want with her?" or "Why are you talking to her?" ²⁸The woman left her water jar beside the well and ran back to the village, telling everyone, ²⁹"Come and see a man who told me everything I ever did! Could he possibly be the Messiah?" ³⁰So the people came streaming from the village to see him.

³¹Meanwhile, the disciples were urging Jesus, "Rabbi, eat something." ³²But Jesus replied, "I have a kind of food you know nothing about."

³³"Did someone bring him food while we were gone?" the disciples asked each other.

³⁴Then Jesus explained: "My nourishment comes from doing the will of God, who sent me, and from finishing his work. ³⁵You know the saying, 'Four months between planting and harvest.' But I say, wake up and look around. The fields are already ripe for harvest. ³⁶The harvesters are paid good wages, and the fruit they harvest is people brought to eternal life. What joy awaits both the planter and the harvester alike! ³⁷You know the saying, 'One plants and another harvests.' And it's true. ³⁸I sent you to harvest where you didn't plant; others had already done the work, and now you will get to gather the harvest."

Many Believe in Jesus

³⁹Many Samaritans from the village believed in Jesus because the woman had said, "He told me everything I ever did!" ⁴⁰When they came out to see him, they begged him to stay in their village. So he stayed for two days, ⁴¹long enough for many more to hear his message and believe. ⁴²Then they said to the woman, "Now we believe, not just because of what you told us, but because we have heard him ourselves. Now we know that he is indeed the Savior of the world."

Jesus Shows His Divine Power

⁴³At the end of the two days, Jesus went on to Galilee. ⁴⁴He himself had said that a prophet is not honored in his own hometown. ⁴⁵Yet the Galileans welcomed him, for they had been in

Jesus is willing to give life to anyone who trusts him. It doesn't matter how sketchy our past may be.

Jerusalem at the Passover celebration and had seen everything he did there.

46As he traveled through Galilee, he came to Cana, where he had turned the water into wine. There was a government official in nearby Capernaum whose son was very sick. 47When he heard that Jesus had come from Judea to Galilee, he went and begged Jesus to come to Capernaum to heal his son, who was about to die.

48Jesus asked, "Will you never believe in me unless you see miraculous signs and wonders?"

49The official pleaded, "Lord, please come now before my little boy dies."

50Then Jesus told him, "Go back home. Your son will live!" And the man believed what Jesus said and started home.

51While the man was on his way, some of his servants met him with the news that his son was alive and well. 52He asked them when the boy had begun to get better, and they replied, "Yesterday afternoon at one o'clock his fever suddenly disappeared!" 53Then the father realized that that was the very time Jesus had told him, "Your son will live." And he and his entire household believed in Jesus. 54This was the second miraculous sign Jesus did in Galilee after coming from Judea.

Jesus Heals a Lame Man

5:1Afterward Jesus returned to Jerusalem for one of the Jewish holy days. 2Inside the city, near the Sheep Gate, was the pool of Bethesda, with five covered porches. 3Crowds of sick people—blind, lame, or paralyzed—lay on the porches. 5One of the men lying there had been sick for thirty-eight years.

6When Jesus saw him and knew he had been ill for a long time, he asked him, "Would you like to get well?"

7"I can't, sir," the sick man said, "for I have no one to put me into the pool when the water bubbles up. Someone else always gets there ahead of me."

8Jesus told him, "Stand up, pick up your mat, and walk!"

9Instantly, the man was healed! He rolled up his sleeping mat and began walking! But this miracle happened on the Sabbath, 10so the Jewish leaders objected. They said to the man who was cured, "You can't work on the Sabbath! The law doesn't allow you to carry that sleeping mat!"

11But he replied, "The man who healed me told me, 'Pick up your mat and walk.'"

12"Who said such a thing as that?" they demanded.

13The man didn't know, for Jesus had disappeared into the crowd. 14But afterward Jesus found him in the Temple and told him, "Now you are well; so stop sinning, or something even worse may happen to you." 15Then the man went and told the Jewish leaders that it was Jesus who had healed him.

Jesus Claims to Be the Son of God

16So the Jewish leaders began harassing Jesus for breaking the Sabbath rules. 17But Jesus replied, "My Father is always working, and so am I." 18So the Jewish leaders tried all the harder to find a way to kill him. For he not only broke the Sabbath, he called God his Father, thereby making himself equal with God.

19So Jesus explained, "I tell you the truth, the Son can do nothing by himself. He does only what he sees the Father doing. Whatever the Father does, the Son also does. ²⁰For the Father loves the Son and shows him everything he is doing. In fact, the Father will show him how to do even the Son of God. And those who listen will live. ²⁶The Father has life in himself, and he has granted that same life-giving power to his Son. ²⁷And he has given him authority to judge everyone because he is the Son of Man. ²⁸Don't be

Jesus is always ready to help those who need it. But he only moves in where he's truly wanted. Don't be too proud or feel too stuck to ask.

greater works than healing this man. Then you will truly be astonished. ²¹For just as the Father gives life to those he raises from the dead, so the Son gives life to anyone he wants. ²²In addition, the Father judges no one. Instead, he has given the Son absolute authority to judge, ²³so that everyone will honor the Son, just as they honor the Father. Anyone who does not honor the Son is certainly not honoring the Father who sent him.

²⁴"I tell you the truth, those who listen to my message and believe in God who sent me have eternal life. They will never be condemned for their sins, but they have already passed from death into life.

²⁵"And I assure you that the time is coming, indeed it's here now, when the dead will hear my voice—the voice of so surprised! Indeed, the time is coming when all the dead in their graves will hear the voice of God's Son, ²⁹and they will rise again. Those who have done good will rise to experience eternal life, and those who have continued in evil will rise to experience judgment. ³⁰I can do nothing on my own. I judge as God tells me. Therefore, my judgment is just, because I carry out the will of the one who sent me, not my own will.

Witnesses to Jesus

³¹"If I were to testify on my own behalf, my testimony would not be valid. ³²But someone else is also testifying about me, and I assure you that everything he says about me is true. ³³In fact, you sent investigators to listen to John the Baptist, and his testimony about me

/// continued on page 19

Jesus Teaches Like No One Else

WHEN THEY CAME DOWN from the mountain, the disciples stood with Jesus on a large, level area, surrounded by many of his followers and by the crowds. There were people from all over Judea and from Jerusalem and from as far north as the seacoasts of Tyre and Sidon. [18]They had come to hear him and to be healed of their diseases; and those troubled by evil spirits were healed. [19]Everyone tried to touch him, because healing power went out from him, and he healed everyone.

Jesus' Upside-Down Kingdom

[20]Then Jesus turned to his disciples and said,

> "God blesses you who are poor,
>   for the Kingdom of God is yours.
> [21] God blesses you who are hungry now,
>   for you will be satisfied.
> God blesses you who weep now,
>   for in due time you will laugh.

[22]What blessings await you when people hate you and exclude you and mock you and curse you as evil because you follow the Son of Man. [23]When that happens, be happy! Yes, leap for joy! For a great reward awaits you in heaven. And remember, their ancestors treated the ancient prophets that same way.

Sorrows For Those Outside Jesus' Kingdom

[24] "What sorrow awaits you who are rich,
>   for you have your only happiness now.
> [25] What sorrow awaits you who are fat and prosperous now,
>   for a time of awful hunger awaits you.
> What sorrow awaits you who laugh now,
>   for your laughing will turn to mourning and sorrow.
> [26] What sorrow awaits you who are praised by the crowds,
>   for their ancestors also praised false prophets.

Jesus is fresh and original. People are blown away by what he says. He makes sense of life's confusion and cuts through religious mysteries.

Love for Enemies

[27]"But to you who are willing to listen, I say, love your enemies! Do good to those who hate you. [28]Bless those who curse you. Pray for those who hurt you. [29]If someone slaps you on one cheek, offer the other cheek also. If someone demands your coat, offer your shirt also. [30]Give to anyone who asks; and when things are taken away from you, don't try to get them back. [31]Do to others as you would like them to do to you.

[32]"If you love only those who love you, why should you get credit for that? Even sinners love those who love them! [33]And if you do good only to those who do good to you, why should you get credit? Even sinners do that much! [34]And if you lend money only to those who can repay you, why should you get credit? Even sinners will lend to other sinners for a full return.

[35]"Love your enemies! Do good to them. Lend to them without expecting to be repaid. Then your reward from heaven will be very great, and you will truly be acting as children of the Most High, for he is kind to those who are unthankful and wicked. [36]You must be compassionate, just as your Father is compassionate.

Do Not Judge Others

[37] "Do not judge others, and you will not be judged. Do not condemn others, or it will all come back against you. Forgive others, and you will be forgiven. [38] Give, and you will receive. Your gift will return to you in full—pressed down, shaken together to make room for more, running over, and poured into your lap. The amount you give will determine the amount you get back."

[39] Then Jesus gave the following illustration: "Can one blind person lead another? Won't they both fall into a ditch? [40] Students are not greater than their teacher. But the student who is fully trained will become like the teacher.

[41] "And why worry about a speck in your friend's eye when you have a log in your own? [42] How can you think of saying, 'Friend, let me help you get rid of that speck in your eye,' when you can't see past the log in your own eye? Hypocrite! First get rid of the log in your own eye; then you will see well enough to deal with the speck in your friend's eye.

The Tree and Its Fruit

[43] "A good tree can't produce bad fruit, and a bad tree can't produce good fruit. [44] A tree is identified by its fruit. Figs are never gathered from thornbushes, and grapes are not picked from bramble bushes. [45] A good person produces good things from the treasury of a good heart, and an evil person produces evil things from the treasury of an evil heart. What you say flows from what is in your heart.

Building on a Solid Foundation

[46] "So why do you keep calling me 'Lord, Lord!' when you don't do what I say? [47] I will show you what it's like when someone comes to me, listens to my teaching, and then follows it. [48] It is like a person building a house who digs deep and lays the foundation on solid rock. When the floodwaters rise and break against that house, it stands firm because it is well built. [49] But anyone who hears and doesn't obey is like a person who builds a house without a foundation. When the floods sweep down against that house, it will collapse into a heap of ruins." ∎

Jesus is not always who we want him to be. But he is always who we need him to be. There's nothing he can't do.

/// continued from page 15

was true. [34]Of course, I have no need of human witnesses, but I say these things so you might be saved. [35]John was like a burning and shining lamp, and you were excited for a while about his message. [36]But I have a greater witness than John—my teachings and my miracles. The Father gave me these works to accomplish, and they prove that he sent me. [37]And the Father who sent me has testified about me himself. You have never heard his voice or seen him face to face, [38]and you do not have his message in your hearts, because you do not believe me—the one he sent to you.

[39]"You search the Scriptures because you think they give you eternal life. But the Scriptures point to me! [40]Yet you refuse to come to me to receive this life.

[41]"Your approval means nothing to me, [42]because I know you don't have God's love within you. [43]For I have come to you in my Father's name, and you have rejected me. Yet if others come in their own name, you gladly welcome them. [44]No wonder you can't believe! For you gladly honor each other, but you don't care about the honor that comes from the one who alone is God.

[45]"Yet it isn't I who will accuse you before the Father. Moses will accuse you! Yes, Moses, in whom you put your hopes. [46]If you really believed Moses, you would believe me, because he wrote about me. [47]But since you don't believe what he wrote, how will you believe what I say?"

Jesus Feeds Five Thousand

[6:1]After this, Jesus crossed over to the far side of the Sea of Galilee, also known as the Sea of Tiberias. [2]A huge crowd kept following him wherever he went, because they saw his miraculous signs as he healed the sick. [3]Then Jesus climbed a hill and sat down with his disciples around him. [4](It was nearly time for the Jewish Passover celebration.) [5]Jesus soon saw a huge crowd of people coming to look for him. Turning to Philip, he asked, "Where can we buy bread to feed all these people?" [6]He was testing Philip, for he already knew what he was going to do.

[7]Philip replied, "Even if we worked for months, we wouldn't have enough money to feed them!"

[8]Then Andrew, Simon Peter's brother, spoke up. [9]"There's a young boy here with five barley loaves and two fish. But what good is that with this huge crowd?"

[10]"Tell everyone to sit down," Jesus said. So they all sat down on the grassy slopes. (The men alone numbered about 5,000.) [11]Then Jesus took the loaves, gave thanks to God, and distributed them to the people. Afterward he did the same with the fish. And they all ate as much as they wanted. [12]After everyone was full, Jesus told his disciples, "Now gather the leftovers, so that nothing is wasted." [13]So they picked up the pieces and filled twelve baskets with scraps left by the people who had eaten from the five barley loaves.

[14]When the people saw him do this miraculous sign, they exclaimed, "Surely, he is the Prophet we have been expecting!" [15]When Jesus saw that they were ready to force him to be their king, he slipped away into the hills by himself.

Jesus Walks on Water

[16]That evening Jesus' disciples went down to the shore to wait for him. [17]But as darkness fell and Jesus still hadn't come back, they got into the boat and headed across the lake toward Capernaum. [18]Soon a gale swept down upon them, and the sea grew very rough. [19]They had rowed three or four miles when suddenly they saw Jesus walking on the water toward the boat. They were terrified, [20]but he called out to them, "Don't be afraid. I am here!" [21]Then they were eager to let him in the boat, and immediately they arrived at their destination!

Jesus' Message Isn't about Easy Religion

[22]The next day the crowd that had stayed on the far shore saw that the disciples had taken the only boat, and they realized Jesus had not gone with them. [23]Several boats from Tiberias landed near the place where the Lord had blessed the bread and the people had eaten. [24]So when the crowd saw that neither Jesus nor his disciples were there, they got into the boats and went across to Capernaum to look for him. [25]They found him on the other side of the lake and asked, "Rabbi, when did you get here?"

[26]Jesus replied, "I tell you the truth, you want to be with me because I fed you, not because you understood the miraculous signs. [27]But don't be so concerned about perishable things like food. Spend your energy seeking the eternal life that the Son of Man can give you. For God the Father has given me the seal of his approval."

[28]They replied, "We want to perform God's works, too. What should we do?"

[29]Jesus told them, "This is the only work God wants from you: Believe in the one he has sent."

[30]They answered, "Show us a

miraculous sign if you want us to believe in you. What can you do? [31]After all, our ancestors ate manna while they journeyed through the wilderness! The Scriptures say, 'Moses gave them bread from heaven to eat.'"

[32]Jesus said, "I tell you the truth, Moses didn't give you bread from heaven. My Father did. And now he offers you the true bread from heaven. [33]The true bread of God is the one who comes down from heaven and gives life to the world."

[34]"Sir," they said, "give us that bread every day."

[35]Jesus replied, "I am the bread of life. Whoever comes to me will never be hungry again. Whoever believes in me will never be thirsty. [36]But you haven't believed in me even though you have seen me. [37]However, those the Father has given me will come to me, and I will never reject them. [38]For I have come down from heaven to do the will of God who sent me, not to do my own will. [39]And this is the will of God, that I should not lose even one of all those he has given me, but that I should raise them up at the last day. [40]For it is my Father's will that all who see his Son and believe in him should have eternal life. I will raise them up at the last day."

[41]Then the people began to murmur in disagreement because he had said, "I am the bread that came down from heaven." [42]They said, "Isn't this Jesus, the son of Joseph? We know his father and mother. How can he say, 'I came down from heaven'?"

[43]But Jesus replied, "Stop complaining about what I said. [44]For no one can come to me unless the Father who sent me draws them to me, and at the last day I will raise them up. [45]As it is written in the Scriptures, 'They will all be taught by God.' Everyone who listens to the Father and learns from him comes to me. [46](Not that anyone has ever seen the Father; only I, who was sent from God, have seen him.)

[47]"I tell you the truth, anyone who believes has eternal life. [48]Yes, I am the bread of life! [49]Your ancestors ate manna in the wilderness, but they all died. [50]Anyone who eats the bread from heaven, however, will never die. [51]I am the living bread that came down from heaven. Anyone who eats this bread will live forever; and this bread, which I will offer so the world may live, is my flesh."

[52]Then the people began arguing with each other about what he meant. "How can this man give us his flesh to eat?" they asked.

[53]So Jesus said again, "I tell you the truth, unless you eat the flesh of the Son of Man and drink his blood, you cannot have eternal life within you. [54]But anyone who eats my flesh

---

Jesus called himself the bread of life—essential for everyone. That raises the question: Do you think of Jesus as life-critical or life-optional?

---

and drinks my blood has eternal life, and I will raise that person at the last day. ⁵⁵For my flesh is true food, and my blood is true drink. ⁵⁶Anyone who eats my flesh and drinks my blood remains in me, and I in him. ⁵⁷I live because of the living Father who sent me; in the same way, anyone who feeds on me will live because of me. ⁵⁸I am the true bread that came down from heaven. Anyone who eats this bread will not die as your ancestors did (even though they ate the manna) but will live forever."

⁵⁹He said these things while he was teaching in the synagogue in Capernaum.

Many Disciples Desert Jesus

⁶⁰Many of his disciples said, "This is very hard to understand. How can anyone accept it?"

⁶¹Jesus was aware that his disciples were complaining, so he said to them, "Does this offend you? ⁶²Then what will you think if you see the Son of Man ascend to heaven again? ⁶³The Spirit alone gives eternal life. Human effort accomplishes nothing. And the very words I have spoken to you are spirit and life. ⁶⁴But some of you do not believe me." (For Jesus knew from the beginning which ones didn't believe, and he knew who would betray him.) ⁶⁵Then he said, "That is why I said that people can't come to me unless the Father gives them to me."

⁶⁶At this point many of his disciples turned away and deserted him. ⁶⁷Then Jesus turned to the Twelve and asked, "Are you also going to leave?"

⁶⁸Simon Peter replied, "Lord, to whom would we go? You have the words that give eternal life. ⁶⁹We believe, and we know you are the Holy One of God."

⁷⁰Then Jesus said, "I chose the twelve of you, but one is a devil." ⁷¹He was speaking of Judas, son of Simon Iscariot, one of the Twelve, who would later betray him.

Jesus and His Brothers

⁷:¹After this, Jesus traveled around Galilee. He wanted to stay out of Judea, where the Jewish leaders were plotting his death. ²But soon it was time for the Jewish Festival of Shelters, ³and Jesus' brothers said to him, "Leave here and go to Judea, where your followers can see your miracles! ⁴You can't become famous if you hide like this! If you can do such wonderful things, show yourself to the world!" ⁵For even his brothers didn't believe in him.

⁶Jesus replied, "Now is not the right time for me to go, but you can go anytime. ⁷The world can't hate you, but it does hate me because I accuse it of doing evil. ⁸You go on. I'm not going to this festival, because my time has not yet come." ⁹After saying these things, Jesus remained in Galilee.

Jesus Teaches Openly at the Temple

¹⁰But after his brothers left for the festival, Jesus also went, though secretly, staying out of public view. ¹¹The Jewish leaders tried to find him at the festival and kept asking if anyone had seen him. ¹²There was a lot of grumbling about him among the crowds. Some argued, "He's a good man," but others said, "He's nothing but a fraud who deceives the people." ¹³But no one had the courage to speak favorably about him

in public, for they were afraid of getting in trouble with the Jewish leaders.

¹⁴Then, midway through the festival, Jesus went up to the Temple and began to teach. ¹⁵The people were surprised when they heard him. "How does he know so much when he hasn't been trained?" they asked.

¹⁶So Jesus told them, "My message is not my own; it comes from God who sent me. ¹⁷Anyone who wants to do the will of God will know whether my teaching is from God or is merely my own. ¹⁸Those who speak for themselves want glory only for themselves, but a person who seeks to honor the one who sent him speaks truth, not lies. ¹⁹Moses gave you the law, but none of you obeys it! In fact, you are trying to kill me."

²⁰The crowd replied, "You're demon possessed! Who's trying to kill you?"

²¹Jesus replied, "I did one miracle on the Sabbath, and you were amazed. ²²But you work on the Sabbath, too, when you obey Moses' law of circumcision. (Actually, this tradition of circumcision began with the patriarchs, long before the law of Moses.) ²³For if the correct time for circumcising your son falls on the Sabbath, you go ahead and do it so as not to break the law of Moses. So why should you be angry with me for healing a man on the Sabbath? ²⁴Look beneath the surface so you can judge correctly."

Is Jesus God's Chosen One?

²⁵Some of the people who lived in Jerusalem started to ask each other, "Isn't this the man they are trying to kill? ²⁶But here he is, speaking in public, and they say nothing to him. Could our leaders possibly believe that he is the Messiah? ²⁷But how could he be? For we know where this man comes from. When the Messiah comes, he will simply appear; no one will know where he comes from."

²⁸While Jesus was teaching in the Temple, he called out, "Yes, you know me, and you know where I come from. But I'm not here on my own. The one who sent me is true, and you don't know him. ²⁹But I know him because I come from him, and he sent me to you." ³⁰Then the leaders tried to arrest him; but no one laid a hand on him, because his time had not yet come.

³¹Many among the crowds at the Temple believed in him. "After all," they said, "would you expect the Messiah to do more miraculous signs than this man has done?"

³²When the Pharisees heard that the crowds were whispering such things, they and the leading priests sent Temple guards to arrest Jesus. ³³But Jesus told them, "I will be with you only a little longer. Then I will return to the one who sent me. ³⁴You will search for me but not find me. And you cannot go where I am going."

³⁵The Jewish leaders were puzzled by this statement. "Where is he planning to go?" they asked. "Is he thinking of leaving the country and going to the Jews in other lands? Maybe he will even teach the Greeks! ³⁶What does he mean when he says, 'You will search for me but not find me,' and 'You cannot go where I am going'?"

Jesus Promises Living Water

³⁷On the last day, the climax of the festival, Jesus stood and shouted to the crowds, "Anyone who is thirsty may

Jesus is the light we need to see what's really important, what's scary dangerous, and how to squeeze the most out of life.

© MARCIN KILARSKI/PHOTOS.COM

come to me! ³⁸Anyone who believes in me may come and drink! For the Scriptures declare, 'Rivers of living water will flow from his heart.'" ³⁹(When he said "living water," he was speaking of the Spirit, who would be given to everyone believing in him. But the Spirit had not yet been given, because Jesus had not yet entered into his glory.)

Division and Unbelief

⁴⁰When the crowds heard him say this, some of them declared, "Surely this man is the Prophet we've been expecting." ⁴¹Others said, "He is the Messiah." Still others said, "But he can't be! Will the Messiah come from Galilee? ⁴²For the Scriptures clearly state that the Messiah will be born of the royal line of David, in Bethlehem, the village where King David was born." ⁴³So the crowd was divided about him. ⁴⁴Some even wanted him arrested, but no one laid a hand on him.

⁴⁵When the Temple guards returned without having arrested Jesus, the leading priests and Pharisees demanded, "Why didn't you bring him in?"

⁴⁶"We have never heard anyone speak like this!" the guards responded.

⁴⁷"Have you been led astray, too?" the Pharisees mocked. ⁴⁸"Is there a single one of us rulers or Pharisees who believes in him? ⁴⁹This foolish crowd follows him, but they are ignorant of the law. God's curse is on them!"

⁵⁰Then Nicodemus, the leader who had met with Jesus earlier, spoke up. ⁵¹"Is it legal to convict a man before he is given a hearing?" he asked.

⁵²They replied, "Are you from Galilee, too? Search the Scriptures and see for yourself—no prophet ever comes from Galilee!"

⁵³Then the meeting broke up, and everybody went home.

Jesus Confronts Religious Leaders

⁸:¹Jesus returned to the Mount of Olives, ²but early the next morning he was back again at the Temple. A crowd soon gathered, and he sat down and

taught them. ³As he was speaking, the teachers of religious law and the Pharisees brought a woman who had been caught in the act of adultery. They put her in front of the crowd.

⁴"Teacher," they said to Jesus, "this woman was caught in the act of adultery. ⁵The law of Moses says to stone her. What do you say?"

⁶They were trying to trap him into saying something they could use against him, but Jesus stooped down and wrote in the dust with his finger. ⁷They kept demanding an answer, so he stood up again and said, "All right, but let the one who has never sinned throw the first stone!" ⁸Then he stooped down again and wrote in the dust.

⁹When the accusers heard this, they slipped away one by one, beginning with the oldest, until only Jesus was left in the middle of the crowd with the woman. ¹⁰Then Jesus stood up again and said to the woman, "Where are your accusers? Didn't even one of them condemn you?"

¹¹"No, Lord," she said.

And Jesus said, "Neither do I. Go and sin no more."

Jesus, the Light of the World

¹²Jesus spoke to the people once more and said, "I am the light of the world. If you follow me, you won't have to walk in darkness, because you will have the light that leads to life."

¹³The Pharisees replied, "You are making those claims about yourself! Such testimony is not valid."

¹⁴Jesus told them, "These claims are valid even though I make them about myself. For I know where I came from and where I am going, but you don't know this about me. ¹⁵You judge me by human standards, but I do not judge anyone. ¹⁶And if I did, my judgment would be correct in every respect because I am not alone. The Father who sent me is with me. ¹⁷Your own law says that if two people agree about something, their witness is accepted as fact. ¹⁸I am one witness, and my Father who sent me is the other."

¹⁹"Where is your father?" they asked.

Jesus answered, "Since you don't know who I am, you don't know who my Father is. If you knew me, you would also know my Father." ²⁰Jesus made these statements while he was teaching in the section of the Temple known as the Treasury. But he was not arrested, because his time had not yet come.

The Unbelieving People Warned

²¹Later Jesus said to them again, "I am going away. You will search for me but will die in your sin. You cannot come where I am going."

²²The people asked, "Is he planning to commit suicide? What does he mean, 'You cannot come where I am going'?"

²³Jesus continued, "You are from below; I am from above. You belong to this world; I do not. ²⁴That is why I said that you will die in your sins; for unless you believe that I Am who I claim to be, you will die in your sins."

²⁵"Who are you?" they demanded.

Jesus replied, "The one I have always claimed to be. ²⁶I have much to say about you and much to condemn, but I won't. For I say only what I have heard from the one who sent me, and he is completely truthful." ²⁷But they still didn't understand that he was talking about his Father.

²⁸So Jesus said, "When you have lifted up the Son of Man on the cross, then you will understand that I Aᴍ he. I do nothing on my own but say only what the Father taught me. ²⁹And the one who sent me is with me—he has not deserted me. For I always do what pleases him." ³⁰Then many who heard him say these things believed in him.

Jesus and Abraham

³¹Jesus said to the people who believed in him, "You are truly my disciples if you remain faithful to my teachings. ³²And you will know the truth, and the truth will set you free."

³³"But we are descendants of Abraham," they said. "We have never been slaves to anyone. What do you mean, 'You will be set free'?"

³⁴Jesus replied, "I tell you the truth, everyone who sins is a slave of sin. ³⁵A slave is not a permanent member of the

you are following the advice of your father."

³⁹"Our father is Abraham!" they declared.

"No," Jesus replied, "for if you were really the children of Abraham, you would follow his example. ⁴⁰Instead, you are trying to kill me because I told you the truth, which I heard from God. Abraham never did such a thing. ⁴¹No, you are imitating your real father."

They replied, "We aren't illegitimate children! God himself is our true Father."

⁴²Jesus told them, "If God were your Father, you would love me, because I have come to you from God. I am not here on my own, but he sent me. ⁴³Why can't you understand what I am saying? It's because you can't even hear me! ⁴⁴For you are the children of your father the devil, and you love to do the evil things he does. He was a murderer from the beginning. He has always hated the truth, because there is no truth in him. When he lies, it is

---

Jesus' teachings liberate us, but only if we obey. Can you imagine becoming truly free by reconstructing your life around a commitment to follow Jesus?

---

family, but a son is part of the family forever. ³⁶So if the Son sets you free, you are truly free. ³⁷Yes, I realize that you are descendants of Abraham. And yet some of you are trying to kill me because there's no room in your hearts for my message. ³⁸I am telling you what I saw when I was with my Father. But

consistent with his character; for he is a liar and the father of lies. ⁴⁵So when I tell you the truth, you just naturally don't believe me! ⁴⁶Which of you can truthfully accuse me of sin? And since I am telling you the truth, why don't you believe me? ⁴⁷Anyone who belongs to God listens gladly to the words of God.

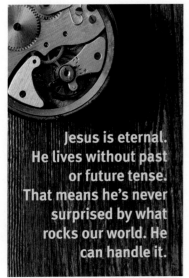

Jesus is eternal. He lives without past or future tense. That means he's never surprised by what rocks our world. He can handle it.

© HAVESEEN/PHOTOS.COM

myself, it doesn't count. But it is my Father who will glorify me. You say, 'He is our God,' ⁵⁵but you don't even know him. I know him. If I said otherwise, I would be as great a liar as you! But I do know him and obey him. ⁵⁶Your father Abraham rejoiced as he looked forward to my coming. He saw it and was glad."

⁵⁷The people said, "You aren't even fifty years old. How can you say you have seen Abraham?"

⁵⁸Jesus answered, "I tell you the truth, before Abraham was even born, I Am!" ⁵⁹At that point they picked up stones to throw at him. But Jesus was hidden from them and left the Temple.

Jesus Heals Physical and Spiritual Blindness

⁹:¹As Jesus was walking along, he saw a man who had been blind from birth. ²"Rabbi," his disciples asked him, "why was this man born blind? Was it because of his own sins or his parents' sins?"

³"It was not because of his sins or his parents' sins," Jesus answered. "This happened so the power of God could be seen in him. ⁴We must quickly carry out the tasks assigned us by the one who sent us. The night is coming, and then no one can work. ⁵But while I am here in the world, I am the light of the world."

⁶Then he spit on the ground, made mud with the saliva, and spread the mud over the blind man's eyes. ⁷He told him, "Go wash yourself in the pool of Siloam" (Siloam means "sent"). So the

But you don't listen because you don't belong to God."

⁴⁸The people retorted, "You Samaritan devil! Didn't we say all along that you were possessed by a demon?"

⁴⁹"No," Jesus said, "I have no demon in me. For I honor my Father—and you dishonor me. ⁵⁰And though I have no wish to glorify myself, God is going to glorify me. He is the true judge. ⁵¹I tell you the truth, anyone who obeys my teaching will never die!"

⁵²The people said, "Now we know you are possessed by a demon. Even Abraham and the prophets died, but you say, 'Anyone who obeys my teaching will never die!' ⁵³Are you greater than our father Abraham? He died, and so did the prophets. Who do you think you are?"

⁵⁴Jesus answered, "If I want glory for

man went and washed and came back seeing!

[8] His neighbors and others who knew him as a blind beggar asked each other, "Isn't this the man who used to sit and beg?" [9] Some said he was, and others said, "No, he just looks like him!"

But the beggar kept saying, "Yes, I am the same one!"

[10] They asked, "Who healed you? What happened?"

[11] He told them, "The man they call Jesus made mud and spread it over my eyes and told me, 'Go to the pool of Siloam and wash yourself.' So I went and washed, and now I can see!"

[12] "Where is he now?" they asked.

"I don't know," he replied.

[13] Then they took the man who had been blind to the Pharisees, [14] because it was on the Sabbath that Jesus had made the mud and healed him. [15] The Pharisees asked the man all about it. So he told them, "He put the mud over my eyes, and when I washed it away, I could see!"

[16] Some of the Pharisees said, "This man Jesus is not from God, for he is working on the Sabbath." Others said, "But how could an ordinary sinner do such miraculous signs?" So there was a deep division of opinion among them.

[17] Then the Pharisees again questioned the man who had been blind and demanded, "What's your opinion about this man who healed you?"

The man replied, "I think he must be a prophet."

[18] The Jewish leaders still refused to believe the man had been blind and could now see, so they called in his parents. [19] They asked them, "Is this your son? Was he born blind? If so, how can he now see?"

[20] His parents replied, "We know this is our son and that he was born blind, [21] but we don't know how he can see or who healed him. Ask him. He is old enough to speak for himself." [22] His parents said this because they were afraid of the Jewish leaders, who had announced that anyone saying Jesus was the Messiah would be expelled from the synagogue. [23] That's why they said, "He is old enough. Ask him."

[24] So for the second time they called in the man who had been blind and told him, "God should get the glory for this, because we know this man Jesus is a sinner."

[25] "I don't know whether he is a sinner," the man replied. "But I know this: I was blind, and now I can see!"

[26] "But what did he do?" they asked. "How did he heal you?"

[27] "Look!" the man exclaimed. "I told you once. Didn't you listen? Why do you want to hear it again? Do you want to become his disciples, too?"

[28] Then they cursed him and said, "You are his disciple, but we are disciples of Moses! [29] We know God spoke to Moses, but we don't even know where this man comes from."

[30] "Why, that's very strange!" the man replied. "He healed my eyes, and yet you don't know where he comes from? [31] We know that God doesn't listen to sinners, but he is ready to hear those who worship him and do his will. [32] Ever since the world began, no one has been able to open the eyes of someone born blind. [33] If this man were not from God, he couldn't have done it."

[34] "You were born a total sinner!"

Jesus is the only hope any of us have to actually see what God created us to see.

they answered. "Are you trying to teach us?" And they threw him out of the synagogue.

Spiritual Blindness

³⁵When Jesus heard what had happened, he found the man and asked, "Do you believe in the Son of Man?"

³⁶The man answered, "Who is he, sir? I want to believe in him."

³⁷"You have seen him," Jesus said, "and he is speaking to you!"

³⁸"Yes, Lord, I believe!" the man said. And he worshiped Jesus.

³⁹Then Jesus told him, "I entered this world to render judgment—to give sight to the blind and to show those who think they see that they are blind."

⁴⁰Some Pharisees who were standing nearby heard him and asked, "Are you saying we're blind?"

⁴¹"If you were blind, you wouldn't be guilty," Jesus replied. "But you remain guilty because you claim you can see.

The Good Shepherd and His Sheep

¹⁰:¹"I tell you the truth, anyone who sneaks over the wall of a sheepfold, rather than going through the gate, must surely be a thief and a robber! ²But the one who enters through the gate is the shepherd of the sheep. ³The gatekeeper opens the gate for him, and the sheep recognize his voice and come to him. He calls his own sheep by name and leads them out. ⁴After he has gathered his own flock, he walks ahead of them, and they follow him because they know his voice. ⁵They won't follow a stranger; they will run from him because they don't know his voice."

⁶Those who heard Jesus use this illustration didn't understand what he meant, ⁷so he explained it to them: "I tell you the truth, I am the gate for the sheep. ⁸All who came before me were thieves and robbers. But the true sheep did not listen to them. ⁹Yes, I am the gate. Those who come in through me will be saved. They will come and go freely and will find good pastures. ¹⁰The thief's purpose is to steal and kill and destroy. My purpose is to give them a rich and satisfying life.

¹¹"I am the good shepherd. The good shepherd sacrifices his life for the

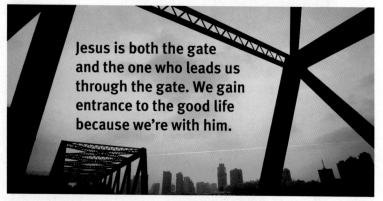

Jesus is both the gate and the one who leads us through the gate. We gain entrance to the good life because we're with him.

sheep. ¹²A hired hand will run when he sees a wolf coming. He will abandon the sheep because they don't belong to him and he isn't their shepherd. And so the wolf attacks them and scatters the flock. ¹³The hired hand runs away because he's working only for the money and doesn't really care about the sheep.

¹⁴"I am the good shepherd; I know my own sheep, and they know me, ¹⁵just as my Father knows me and I know the Father. So I sacrifice my life for the sheep. ¹⁶I have other sheep, too, that are not in this sheepfold. I must bring them also. They will listen to my voice, and there will be one flock with one shepherd.

¹⁷"The Father loves me because I sacrifice my life so I may take it back again. ¹⁸No one can take my life from me. I sacrifice it voluntarily. For I have the authority to lay it down when I want to and also to take it up again. For this is what my Father has commanded."

¹⁹When he said these things, the people were again divided in their opinions about him. ²⁰Some said, "He's demon possessed and out of his mind. Why listen to a man like that?" ²¹Others said, "This doesn't sound like a man possessed by a demon! Can a demon open the eyes of the blind?"

Jesus Claims to Be the Son of God

²²It was now winter, and Jesus was in Jerusalem at the time of Hanukkah, the Festival of Dedication. ²³He was in the Temple, walking through the section known as Solomon's Colonnade. ²⁴The people surrounded him and asked, "How long are you going to keep us in suspense? If you are the Messiah, tell us plainly."

²⁵Jesus replied, "I have already told you, and you don't believe me. The proof is the work I do in my Father's name. ²⁶But you don't believe me because you are not my sheep. ²⁷My sheep listen to my voice; I know them, and they follow me. ²⁸I give them eternal life, and they will never perish. No one can snatch them away from me, ²⁹for my Father has given them to me, and he is more powerful than anyone else. No one can snatch them from the Father's hand. ³⁰The Father and I are one."

³¹Once again the people picked up stones to kill him. ³²Jesus said, "At my Father's direction I have done many good works. For which one are you going to stone me?"

³³They replied, "We're stoning you not for any good work, but for blasphemy! You, a mere man, claim to be God."

³⁴Jesus replied, "It is written in your own Scriptures that God said to certain leaders of the people, 'I say, you are gods!' ³⁵And you know that the Scriptures cannot be altered. So if those people who received God's message were called 'gods,' ³⁶why do you call it blasphemy when I say, 'I am the Son of God'? After all, the Father set me apart and sent me into the world. ³⁷Don't believe me unless I carry out my Father's work. ³⁸But if I do his work, believe in the evidence of the miraculous works I have done, even if you don't believe me. Then you will know and understand that the Father is in me, and I am in the Father."

³⁹Once again they tried to arrest him, but he got away and left them. ⁴⁰He went beyond the Jordan River near the

/// *continued on page 35*

Jesus Reveals God's Heart for Lost Causes

A LARGE CROWD WAS FOLLOWING JESUS. He turned around and said to them, [26] "If you want to be my disciple, you must hate everyone else by comparison—your father and mother, wife and children, brothers and sisters—yes, even your own life. Otherwise, you cannot be my disciple. [27] And if you do not carry your own cross and follow me, you cannot be my disciple.

[28] "But don't begin until you count the cost. For who would begin construction of a building without first calculating the cost to see if there is enough money to finish it? [29] Otherwise, you might complete only the foundation before running out of money, and then everyone would laugh at you. [30] They would say, 'There's the person who started that building and couldn't afford to finish it!'

[31] "Or what king would go to war against another king without first sitting down with his counselors to discuss whether his army of 10,000 could defeat the 20,000 soldiers marching against him? [32] And if he can't, he will send a delegation to discuss terms of peace while the enemy is still far away. [33] So you cannot become my disciple without giving up everything you own.

[34] "Salt is good for seasoning. But if it loses its flavor, how do you make it salty again? [35] Flavorless salt is good neither for the soil nor for the manure pile. It is thrown away. Anyone with ears to hear should listen and understand!"

Story about a Lost Sheep

[15:1] Tax collectors and other notorious sinners often came to listen to Jesus teach. [2] This made the Pharisees and teachers of religious law complain that he was associating with such sinful people—even eating with them!

[3] So Jesus told them this story: [4] "If a man has a hundred sheep and one of them gets lost, what will he do? Won't he leave the ninety-nine others in the wilderness and go to search for the one that is

lost until he finds it? ⁵And when he has found it, he will joyfully carry it home on his shoulders. ⁶When he arrives, he will call together his friends and neighbors, saying, 'Rejoice with me because I have found my lost sheep.' ⁷In the same way, there is more joy in heaven over one lost sinner who repents and returns to God than over ninety-nine others who are righteous and haven't strayed away!

Story about a Lost Coin

⁸"Or suppose a woman has ten silver coins and loses one. Won't she light a lamp and sweep the entire house and search carefully until she finds it? ⁹And when she finds it, she will call in her friends and neighbors and say, 'Rejoice with me because I have found my lost coin.' ¹⁰In the same way, there is joy in the presence of God's angels when even one sinner repents."

Story about the Lost Son

¹¹To illustrate the point further, Jesus told them this story: "A man had two sons. ¹²The younger son told his father, 'I want my share of your estate now before you die.' So his father agreed to divide his wealth between his sons.

¹³"A few days later this younger son packed all his belongings and moved to a distant land, and there he wasted all his money in wild living. ¹⁴About the time his money ran out, a great famine swept over the land, and he began to starve. ¹⁵He persuaded a local farmer to hire him, and the man sent him into his fields to feed the

pigs. ¹⁶The young man became so hungry that even the pods he was feeding the pigs looked good to him. But no one gave him anything.

¹⁷"When he finally came to his senses, he said to himself, 'At home even the hired servants have food enough to spare, and here I am dying of hunger! ¹⁸I will go home to my father and say, "Father, I have sinned against both heaven and you, ¹⁹and I am no longer worthy of being called your son. Please take me on as a hired servant."'

²⁰"So he returned home to his father. And while he was still a long way off, his father saw him coming. Filled with love and compassion, he ran to his son, embraced him, and kissed him. ²¹His son said to him, 'Father, I have sinned against both heaven and you, and I am no longer worthy of being called your son.'

²²"But his father said to the servants, 'Quick! Bring the finest robe in the house and put it on him. Get a ring for his finger and sandals for his feet. ²³And kill the calf we have been fattening. We must celebrate with a feast, ²⁴for this son of mine was dead and has now returned to life. He was lost, but now he is found.' So the party began.

²⁵"Meanwhile, the older son was in the fields working. When he returned home, he heard music and dancing in the house, ²⁶and he asked one of the servants what was going on. ²⁷'Your brother is back,' he was told, 'and your father has killed the fattened calf. We are celebrating because of his safe return.'

²⁸"The older brother was angry and wouldn't go in. His father came out and begged him, ²⁹but he replied, 'All these years I've slaved for you and never once refused to do a single thing you told me to. And in all that time you never gave me even one young goat for a feast with my friends. ³⁰Yet when this son of yours comes back after squandering your money on prostitutes, you celebrate by killing the fattened calf!'

³¹"His father said to him, 'Look, dear son, you have always stayed by me, and everything I have is yours. ³²We had to celebrate this happy day. For your brother was dead and has come back to life! He was lost, but now he is found!'" ∎

place where John was first baptizing and stayed there awhile. ⁴¹And many followed him. "John didn't perform miraculous signs," they remarked to one another, "but everything he said about this man has come true." ⁴²And many who were there believed in Jesus.

Death Is No Match for Jesus

¹¹:¹A man named Lazarus was sick. He lived in Bethany with his sisters, Mary and Martha. ²This is the Mary who later poured the expensive perfume on the Lord's feet and wiped them with her hair. Her brother, Lazarus, was sick. ³So the two sisters sent a message to Jesus telling him, "Lord, your dear friend is very sick."

⁴But when Jesus heard about it he said, "Lazarus's sickness will not end in death. No, it happened for the glory of God so that the Son of God will receive glory from this." ⁵So although Jesus loved Martha, Mary, and Lazarus, ⁶he stayed where he was for the next two days. ⁷Finally, he said to his disciples, "Let's go back to Judea."

⁸But his disciples objected. "Rabbi," they said, "only a few days ago the people in Judea were trying to stone you. Are you going there again?"

⁹Jesus replied, "There are twelve hours of daylight every day. During the day people can walk safely. They can see because they have the light of this world. ¹⁰But at night there is danger of stumbling because they have no light." ¹¹Then he said, "Our friend Lazarus has fallen asleep, but now I will go and wake him up."

¹²The disciples said, "Lord, if he is sleeping, he will soon get better!" ¹³They thought Jesus meant Lazarus was simply sleeping, but Jesus meant Lazarus had died.

¹⁴So he told them plainly, "Lazarus is dead. ¹⁵And for your sakes, I'm glad I wasn't there, for now you will really believe. Come, let's go see him."

¹⁶Thomas, nicknamed the Twin, said to his fellow disciples, "Let's go, too—and die with Jesus."

¹⁷When Jesus arrived at Bethany, he was told that Lazarus had already been in his grave for four days. ¹⁸Bethany was only a few miles down the road from Jerusalem, ¹⁹and many of the people had come to console Martha and Mary in their loss. ²⁰When Martha got word that Jesus was coming, she went to meet him. But Mary stayed in the house. ²¹Martha said to Jesus, "Lord, if only you had been here, my brother would not have died. ²²But even now I know that God will give you whatever you ask."

²³Jesus told her, "Your brother will rise again."

²⁴"Yes," Martha said, "he will rise when everyone else rises, at the last day."

²⁵Jesus told her, "I am the resurrection and the life. Anyone who believes in me will live, even after dying. ²⁶Everyone who lives in me and believes in me will never ever die. Do you believe this, Martha?"

²⁷"Yes, Lord," she told him. "I have always believed you are the Messiah, the Son of God, the one who has come into the world from God." ²⁸Then she

Jesus is life itself. Everywhere. All the time. When he says so, death has to step away from us—regardless of how long we've been corpses.

returned to Mary. She called Mary aside from the mourners and told her, "The Teacher is here and wants to see you." ²⁹So Mary immediately went to him.

³⁰Jesus had stayed outside the village, at the place where Martha met him. ³¹When the people who were at the house consoling Mary saw her leave so hastily, they assumed she was going to Lazarus's grave to weep. So they followed her there. ³²When Mary arrived and saw Jesus, she fell at his feet and said, "Lord, if only you had been here, my brother would not have died."

³³When Jesus saw her weeping and saw the other people wailing with her,

a deep anger welled up within him, and he was deeply troubled. ³⁴"Where have you put him?" he asked them.

They told him, "Lord, come and see." ³⁵Then Jesus wept. ³⁶The people who were standing nearby said, "See how much he loved him!" ³⁷But some said, "This man healed a blind man. Couldn't he have kept Lazarus from dying?"

³⁸Jesus was still angry as he arrived at the tomb, a cave with a stone rolled across its entrance. ³⁹"Roll the stone aside," Jesus told them.

But Martha, the dead man's sister, protested, "Lord, he has been dead for four days. The smell will be terrible."

⁴⁰Jesus responded, "Didn't I tell you that you would see God's glory if you believe?" ⁴¹So they rolled the stone aside. Then Jesus looked up to heaven and said, "Father, thank you for hearing me. ⁴²You always hear me, but I said it out loud for the sake of all these people standing here, so that they will believe you sent me." ⁴³Then Jesus shouted, "Lazarus, come out!" ⁴⁴And the dead man came out, his hands and feet bound in graveclothes, his face wrapped in a headcloth. Jesus told them, "Unwrap him and let him go!"

The Plot to Kill Jesus

⁴⁵Many of the people who were with Mary believed in Jesus when they saw this happen. ⁴⁶But some went to the Pharisees and told them what Jesus had done. ⁴⁷Then the leading priests and Pharisees called the high council together. "What are we going to do?" they asked each other. "This man certainly performs many miraculous signs. ⁴⁸If we allow him to go on like

© GRANDEDUC/PHOTOS.COM

this, soon everyone will believe in him. Then the Roman army will come and destroy both our Temple and our nation."

⁴⁹Caiaphas, who was high priest at that time, said, "You don't know what you're talking about! ⁵⁰You don't realize that it's better for you that one man should die for the people than for the whole nation to be destroyed."

⁵¹He did not say this on his own; as high priest at that time he was led to prophesy that Jesus would die for the entire nation. ⁵²And not only for that nation, but to bring together and unite all the children of God scattered around the world.

⁵³So from that time on, the Jewish leaders began to plot Jesus' death. ⁵⁴As a result, Jesus stopped his public ministry among the people and left Je-

⁵⁷Meanwhile, the leading priests and Pharisees had publicly ordered that anyone seeing Jesus must report it immediately so they could arrest him.

Jesus Is Celebrated, but Not by Everyone

¹²:¹Six days before the Passover celebration began, Jesus arrived in Bethany, the home of Lazarus—the man he had raised from the dead. ²A dinner was prepared in Jesus' honor. Martha served, and Lazarus was among those who ate with him. ³Then Mary took a twelve-ounce jar of expensive perfume made from essence of nard, and she anointed Jesus' feet with it, wiping his feet with her hair. The house was filled with the fragrance.

It certainly has been dangerous to follow Jesus in particular places and times throughout history. Have you thought about what it might cost you to follow him?

rusalem. He went to a place near the wilderness, to the village of Ephraim, and stayed there with his disciples.

⁵⁵It was now almost time for the Jewish Passover celebration, and many people from all over the country arrived in Jerusalem several days early so they could go through the purification ceremony before Passover began. ⁵⁶They kept looking for Jesus, but as they stood around in the Temple, they said to each other, "What do you think? He won't come for Passover, will he?"

⁴But Judas Iscariot, the disciple who would soon betray him, said, ⁵"That perfume was worth a year's wages. It should have been sold and the money given to the poor." ⁶Not that he cared for the poor—he was a thief, and since he was in charge of the disciples' money, he often stole some for himself.

⁷Jesus replied, "Leave her alone. She did this in preparation for my burial. ⁸You will always have the poor among you, but you will not always have me."

/// continued on page 41

Jesus Challenges Wealth and Power

O NCE A RELIGIOUS LEADER asked Jesus this question: "Good Teacher, what should I do to inherit eternal life?" [19]"Why do you call me good?" Jesus asked him. "Only God is truly good. [20]But to answer your question, you know the commandments: 'You must not commit adultery. You must not murder. You must not steal. You must not testify falsely. Honor your father and mother.'"

[21]The man replied, "I've obeyed all these commandments since I was young."

[22]When Jesus heard his answer, he said, "There is still one thing you haven't done. Sell all your possessions and give the money to the poor, and you will have treasure in heaven. Then come, follow me."

[23]But when the man heard this he became very sad, for he was very rich.

[24]When Jesus saw this, he said, "How hard it is for the rich to enter the Kingdom of God! [25]In fact, it is easier for a camel to go through the eye of a needle than for a rich person to enter the Kingdom of God!"

[26]Those who heard this said, "Then who in the world can be saved?"

[27]He replied, "What is impossible for people is possible with God."

[28]Peter said, "We've left our homes to follow you."

[29]"Yes," Jesus replied, "and I assure you that everyone who has given up house or wife or brothers or parents or children, for the sake of the Kingdom of God, [30]will be repaid many times over in this life, and will have eternal life in the world to come."

Jesus Predicts His Death
[31]Taking the twelve disciples aside, Jesus said, "Listen, we're going

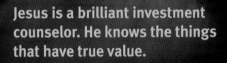

Jesus is a brilliant investment counselor. He knows the things that have true value.

up to Jerusalem, where all the predictions of the prophets concern-ing the Son of Man will come true. ³²He will be handed over to the Romans, and he will be mocked, treated shamefully, and spit upon. ³³They will flog him with a whip and kill him, but on the third day he will rise again."

³⁴But they didn't understand any of this. The significance of his words was hidden from them, and they failed to grasp what he was talking about.

Jesus Heals a Blind Beggar

³⁵As Jesus approached Jericho, a blind beggar was sitting beside the road. ³⁶When he heard the noise of a crowd going past, he asked what was happening. ³⁷They told him that Jesus the Naza-rene was going by. ³⁸So he began shouting, "Jesus, Son of David, have mercy on me!"

³⁹"Be quiet!" the people in front yelled at him.

But he only shouted louder, "Son of David, have mercy on me!" ⁴⁰When Jesus heard him, he stopped and ordered that the man be brought to him. As the man came near, Jesus asked him, ⁴¹"What do you want me to do for you?"

"Lord," he said, "I want to see!"

⁴²And Jesus said, "All right, receive your sight! Your faith has healed you." ⁴³Instantly the man could see, and he followed Jesus, praising God. And all who saw it praised God, too.

Jesus and Zacchaeus

¹⁹:¹Jesus entered Jericho and made his way through the town. ²There was a man there named Zacchaeus. He was the chief tax collector in the region, and he had become very rich. ³He tried to get a look at Jesus, but he was too short to see over the crowd. ⁴So he ran ahead and climbed a sycamore-fig tree beside the road, for Jesus was going to pass that way.

⁵When Jesus came by, he looked up at Zacchaeus and called him by name. "Zacchaeus!" he said. "Quick, come down! I must be a guest in your home today."

⁶Zacchaeus quickly climbed down and took Jesus to his house in great excitement and joy. ⁷But the people were displeased. "He has gone to be the guest of a notorious sinner," they grumbled.

⁸Meanwhile, Zacchaeus stood before the Lord and said, "I will give half my wealth to the poor, Lord, and if I have cheated people on their taxes, I will give them back four times as much!"

⁹Jesus responded, "Salvation has come to this home today, for this man has shown himself to be a true son of Abraham. ¹⁰For the Son of Man came to seek and save those who are lost." ∎

/// continued from page 37

9When all the people heard of Jesus' arrival, they flocked to see him and also to see Lazarus, the man Jesus had raised from the dead. 10Then the leading priests decided to kill Lazarus, too, 11for it was because of him that many of the people had deserted them and believed in Jesus.

Jesus Enters Jerusalem with Fanfare

12The next day, the news that Jesus was on the way to Jerusalem swept through the city. A large crowd of Passover visitors 13took palm branches and went down the road to meet him. They shouted,

"Praise God!
Blessings on the one who comes in
    the name of the Lord!
Hail to the King of Israel!"

14Jesus found a young donkey and rode on it, fulfilling the prophecy that said:

17Many in the crowd had seen Jesus call Lazarus from the tomb, raising him from the dead, and they were telling others about it. 18That was the reason so many went out to meet him—because they had heard about this miraculous sign. 19Then the Pharisees said to each other, "There's nothing we can do. Look, everyone has gone after him!"

Jesus Predicts His Death

20Some Greeks who had come to Jerusalem for the Passover celebration 21paid a visit to Philip, who was from Bethsaida in Galilee. They said, "Sir, we want to meet Jesus." 22Philip told Andrew about it, and they went together to ask Jesus.

23Jesus replied, "Now the time has come for the Son of Man to enter into his glory. 24I tell you the truth, unless a kernel of wheat is planted in the soil and dies, it remains alone. But its death

Burying yourself in Jesus brings new life. It's like you undergo a total identity makeover. How do you think Jesus will reshape you if you choose to follow him?

15 "Don't be afraid, people of
    Jerusalem.
Look, your King is coming,
    riding on a donkey's colt."

16His disciples didn't understand at the time that this was a fulfillment of prophecy. But after Jesus entered into his glory, they remembered what had happened and realized that these things had been written about him.

will produce many new kernels—a plentiful harvest of new lives. 25Those who love their life in this world will lose it. Those who care nothing for their life in this world will keep it for eternity. 26Anyone who wants to serve me must follow me, because my servants must be where I am. And the Father will honor anyone who serves me. 27"Now my soul is deeply troubled.

Should I pray, 'Father, save me from this hour'? But this is the very reason I came! ²⁸Father, bring glory to your name."

Then a voice spoke from heaven, saying, "I have already brought glory to my name, and I will do so again." ²⁹When the crowd heard the voice, for you just a little longer. Walk in the light while you can, so the darkness will not overtake you. Those who walk in the darkness cannot see where they are going. ³⁶Put your trust in the light while there is still time; then you will become children of the light."

After saying these things, Jesus went

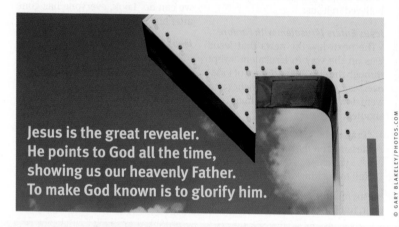

Jesus is the great revealer. He points to God all the time, showing us our heavenly Father. To make God known is to glorify him.

some thought it was thunder, while others declared an angel had spoken to him.

³⁰Then Jesus told them, "The voice was for your benefit, not mine. ³¹The time for judging this world has come, when Satan, the ruler of this world, will be cast out. ³²And when I am lifted up from the earth, I will draw everyone to myself." ³³He said this to indicate how he was going to die.

³⁴The crowd responded, "We understood from Scripture that the Messiah would live forever. How can you say the Son of Man will die? Just who is this Son of Man, anyway?"

³⁵Jesus replied, "My light will shine away and was hidden from them.

The Unbelief of the People

³⁷But despite all the miraculous signs Jesus had done, most of the people still did not believe in him. ³⁸This is exactly what Isaiah the prophet had predicted:

"LORD, who has believed our
message?
To whom has the LORD revealed
his powerful arm?"

³⁹But the people couldn't believe, for as Isaiah also said,

⁴⁰ "The Lord has blinded their eyes
and hardened their hearts—
so that their eyes cannot see,

and their hearts cannot
understand,
and they cannot turn to me
and have me heal them."

⁴¹Isaiah was referring to Jesus when he said this, because he saw the future and spoke of the Messiah's glory. ⁴²Many people did believe in him, however, including some of the Jewish leaders. But they wouldn't admit it for fear that the Pharisees would expel them from the synagogue. ⁴³For they loved human praise more than the praise of God.

⁴⁴Jesus shouted to the crowds, "If you trust me, you are trusting not only me, but also God who sent me. ⁴⁵For when you see me, you are seeing the one who sent me. ⁴⁶I have come as a light to shine in this dark world, so that all who put their trust in me will no longer remain in the dark. ⁴⁷I will not judge those who hear me but don't obey me, for I have come to save the world and not to judge it. ⁴⁸But all who reject me and my message will be judged on the day of judgment by the truth I have spoken. ⁴⁹I don't speak on my own authority. The Father who sent me has commanded me what to say and how to say it. ⁵⁰And I know his commands lead to eternal life; so I say whatever the Father tells me to say."

Jesus' Disciples Still Don't Understand

13 ¹Before the Passover celebration, Jesus knew that his hour had come to leave this world and return to his Father. He had loved his disciples during his ministry on earth, and now he loved them to the very end. ²It was time for supper, and the devil had already prompted Judas, son of Simon Iscariot, to betray Jesus. ³Jesus knew that the Father had given him authority over everything and that he had come from God and would return to God. ⁴So he got up from the table, took off his robe, wrapped a towel around his waist, ⁵and poured water into a basin. Then he began to wash the disciples' feet, drying them with the towel he had around him.

⁶When Jesus came to Simon Peter, Peter said to him, "Lord, are you going to wash my feet?"

⁷Jesus replied, "You don't understand now what I am doing, but someday you will."

⁸"No," Peter protested, "you will never ever wash my feet!"

Jesus replied, "Unless I wash you, you won't belong to me."

⁹Simon Peter exclaimed, "Then wash my hands and head as well, Lord, not just my feet!"

¹⁰Jesus replied, "A person who has bathed all over does not need to wash, except for the feet, to be entirely clean. And you disciples are clean, but not all of you." ¹¹For Jesus knew who would betray him. That is what he meant when he said, "Not all of you are clean."

¹²After washing their feet, he put on his robe again and sat down and asked, "Do you understand what I was doing? ¹³You call me 'Teacher' and 'Lord,' and you are right, because that's what I am. ¹⁴And since I, your Lord and Teacher,

Jesus is a person unlike the world has ever seen. In him immeasurable power was combined with complete humility and service—for us.

have washed your feet, you ought to wash each other's feet. [15] I have given you an example to follow. Do as I have done to you. [16] I tell you the truth, slaves are not greater than their master. Nor is the messenger more important than the one who sends the message. [17] Now that you know these things, God will bless you for doing them.

Jesus Predicts His Betrayal

[18] "I am not saying these things to all of you; I know the ones I have chosen. But this fulfills the Scripture that says, 'The one who eats my food has turned against me.' [19] I tell you this beforehand, so that when it happens you will believe that I AM the Messiah. [20] I tell you the truth, anyone who welcomes my messenger is welcoming me, and anyone who welcomes me is welcoming the Father who sent me."

[21] Now Jesus was deeply troubled, and he exclaimed, "I tell you the truth, one of you will betray me!"

[22] The disciples looked at each other, wondering whom he could mean. [23] The disciple Jesus loved was sitting next to Jesus at the table. [24] Simon Peter motioned to him to ask, "Who's he talking about?" [25] So that disciple leaned over to Jesus and asked, "Lord, who is it?"

[26] Jesus responded, "It is the one to whom I give the bread I dip in the bowl." And when he had dipped it, he gave it to Judas, son of Simon Iscariot. [27] When Judas had eaten the bread, Satan entered into him. Then Jesus told him, "Hurry and do what you're going to do." [28] None of the others at the table knew what Jesus meant. [29] Since Judas was their treasurer, some thought Jesus was telling him to go and pay for the

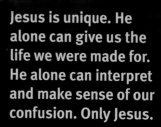

Jesus is unique. He alone can give us the life we were made for. He alone can interpret and make sense of our confusion. Only Jesus.

food or to give some money to the poor. [30] So Judas left at once, going out into the night.

Jesus Predicts Peter's Denial

[31] As soon as Judas left the room, Jesus said, "The time has come for the Son of Man to enter into his glory, and God will be glorified because of him. [32] And since God receives glory because of the Son, he will give his own glory to the Son, and he will do so at once. [33] Dear children, I will be with you only a little longer. And as I told the Jewish leaders, you will search for me, but you can't come where I am going. [34] So now I am giving you a new commandment: Love each other. Just as I have loved you, you should love each other. [35] Your love for

one another will prove to the world that you are my disciples."

[36] Simon Peter asked, "Lord, where are you going?"

And Jesus replied, "You can't go with me now, but you will follow me later."

[37] "But why can't I come now, Lord?" he asked. "I'm ready to die for you."

[38] Jesus answered, "Die for me? I tell you the truth, Peter—before the rooster crows tomorrow morning, you will deny three times that you even know me.

Jesus Assures His Disciples that They Can Trust Him

[14:1] "Don't let your hearts be troubled. Trust in God, and trust also in me. [2] There is more than enough room in my Father's home. If this were not so, would I have told you that I am going to prepare a place for you? [3] When everything is ready, I will come and get you, so that you will always be with me where I am. [4] And you know the way to where I am going."

[5] "No, we don't know, Lord," Thomas said. "We have no idea where you are going, so how can we know the way?"

[6] Jesus told him, "I am the way, the truth, and the life. No one can come to the Father except through me. [7] If you had really known me, you would know who my Father is. From now on, you do know him and have seen him!"

[8] Philip said, "Lord, show us the Father, and we will be satisfied."

[9] Jesus replied, "Have I been with you all this time, Philip, and yet you still don't know who I am? Anyone who has seen me has seen the Father! So why are you asking me to show him to you? [10] Don't you believe that I am in the Father and the Father is in me? The words I speak are not my own, but my Father who lives in me does his work through me. [11] Just believe that I am in the Father and the Father is in me. Or at least believe because of the work you have seen me do.

[12] "I tell you the truth, anyone who believes in me will do the same works I have done, and even greater works, because I am going to be with the Father. [13] You can ask for anything in my name, and I will do it, so that the Son can bring glory to the Father. [14] Yes, ask me for anything in my name, and I will do it!

Those who decide to follow Jesus will never be left to figure it out alone. What difference does it make to you that the Holy Spirit is always present to guide you?

Jesus Promises the Holy Spirit

[15] "If you love me, obey my commandments. [16] And I will ask the Father, and he will give you another Advocate, who will never leave you. [17] He is the Holy Spirit, who leads into all truth. The world cannot receive him, because it

isn't looking for him and doesn't recognize him. But you know him, because he lives with you now and later will be in you. ¹⁸No, I will not abandon you as orphans—I will come to you. ¹⁹Soon the world will no longer see me, but you will see me. Since I live, you also will live. ²⁰When I am raised to life again, you will know that I am in my Father, and you are in me, and I am in you. ²¹Those who accept my commandments and obey them are the ones who love me. And because they love me, my Father will love them. And I will love them and reveal myself to each of them."

²²Judas (not Judas Iscariot, but the other disciple with that name) said to him, "Lord, why are you going to reveal yourself only to us and not to the world at large?"

²³Jesus replied, "All who love me will do what I say. My Father will love them, and we will come and make our home with each of them. ²⁴Anyone who doesn't love me will not obey me. And remember, my words are not my own. What I am telling you is from the Father who sent me. ²⁵I am telling you these things now while I am still with you. ²⁶But when the Father sends the Advocate as my representative—that is, the Holy Spirit—he will teach you everything and will remind you of everything I have told you.

²⁷"I am leaving you with a gift—peace of mind and heart. And the peace I give is a gift the world cannot give. So don't be troubled or afraid. ²⁸Remember what I told you: I am going away, but I will come back to you again. If you really loved me, you would be happy that I am going to the Father, who is greater than I am. ²⁹I have told you these things before they happen so that when they do happen, you will believe.

³⁰"I don't have much more time to talk to you, because the ruler of this world approaches. He has no power over me, ³¹but I will do what the Father requires of me, so that the world will know that I love the Father. Come, let's be going.

Jesus, the True Vine

¹⁵:¹"I am the true grapevine, and my Father is the gardener. ²He cuts off every branch of mine that doesn't produce fruit, and he prunes the branches that do bear fruit so they will produce even more. ³You have already been pruned and purified by the message I have given you. ⁴Remain in me, and I will remain in you. For a branch cannot produce fruit if it is severed from the vine, and you cannot be fruitful unless you remain in me.

⁵"Yes, I am the vine; you are the branches. Those who remain in me, and I in them, will produce much fruit. For apart from me you can do nothing. ⁶Anyone who does not remain in me is thrown away like a useless branch and withers. Such branches are gathered into a pile to be burned. ⁷But if you remain in me and my words remain in you, you may ask for anything you want, and it will be granted! ⁸When you produce much fruit, you are my true disciples. This brings great glory to my Father.

⁹"I have loved you even as the Father has loved me. Remain in my love. ¹⁰When you obey my commandments, you remain in my love, just as I obey my Father's commandments and remain in

his love. [11] I have told you these things so that you will be filled with my joy. Yes, your joy will overflow! [12] This is my commandment: Love each other in the same way I have loved you. [13] There is no greater love than to lay down one's life for one's friends. [14] You are my friends if you do what I command. [15] I no longer call you slaves, because a master doesn't confide in his slaves. Now you are my friends, since I have told you everything the Father told me. [16] You didn't choose me. I chose you. I appointed you to go and produce lasting fruit, so that the Father will give you whatever you ask for, using my name. [17] This is my command: Love each other.

The World Hates Jesus and His Followers

[18] "If the world hates you, remember that it hated me first. [19] The world would love you as one of its own if you belonged to it, but you are no longer part of the world. I chose you to come out of the world, so it hates you. [20] Do you remember what I told you? 'A slave is not greater than the master.' Since they persecuted me, naturally they will persecute you. And if they had listened to me, they would listen to you. [21] They will do all this to you because of me, for they have rejected the one who sent me. [22] They would not be guilty if I had not come and spoken to them. But now they have no excuse for their sin. [23] Anyone who hates me also hates my Father. [24] If I hadn't done such miraculous signs among them that no one else could do, they would not be guilty. But as it is, they have seen everything I did, yet they still hate me and my Father. [25] This fulfills what is written in their Scriptures: 'They hated me without cause.'

[26] "But I will send you the Advocate—the Spirit of truth. He will come to you from the Father and will testify all about me. [27] And you must also testify

> **Jesus is the source of everything in life that qualifies as worthwhile fruit. Connecting to him is how we really live.**

Remain

Have you ever been on a tandem bike? At first it might seem as if it would be easier to ride a bike with the help of another person pumping the pedals behind you, but it doesn't take long to realize it's not that easy to steer a tandem. Maneuvering around obstacles is tricky while both bikers try to pedal in sync. But if you ride with someone who has tandem bike experience, knows how to navigate scary curves and bumpy terrain, and even knows some shortcuts in the route, you would be wise to let that person take the handle-bars. *"Pedal, hang on, and enjoy the ride"* are his instructions. In fact, your biggest role is just to remain on the bike. If you *remain* he can handle the rest.

Jesus calls us to *remain*. He offers all we need to live life to the fullest, and to do that he tells us, *"Remain* in me." It isn't that he is self-centered or controlling, but he knows the way for us to live life as God intended. He even promises to meet our every need when we choose to *remain* with him. Just like the biker, he knows how to get us through the scary and bumpy places in life and show us an adventure like we've never known before. Hold on, don't let go, don't leave, stay put. *"Remain"* is Jesus' big instruction to us. After all, doesn't it make sense that, as the creator of life, Jesus Chris

WHAT DOES REMAIN MEAN IN JOHN 15?

Jesus uses the word *remain* ten times in this speech, so it must be a big deal. He wants his followers to *remain* with him all the time. Only Jesus can give us the spiritual nourishment we need to live to the fullest. Since Jesus constantly *remains* with his Father God, when we *remain* in Jesus we connect to the Father, too. God's ongoing story includes the storyline contributions we make as we remain in Christ.

As Jesus is saying these things, he is spending some of his final moments with his closest friends. They share a meal together and then walk through a vineyard. While walking, Jesus observes that a branch can only produce grapes when it remains connected to the main vine. He drives home the point that we will only be able to produce life kind of fruit that looks like Jesus when we remain connected to Jesus. We can't generate that kind of fruit on our own. God does the work in us when we remain in him— just as it works with grapes, branches and vines.

■ *In order for a lamp to shine, the light bulb must remain in the fixture.*

■ *Remain within coverage areas to use cell phones.*

■ *A fish that wants to breathe must remain underwater.*

■ *A baby remains in the care of her parents to receive life-giving nourishment.*

The experience of remaining in Christ is critically important. So important that Jesus said, "Apart from me you can do nothing" (John 15:5). Jesus wants us to produce good fruit and make a difference in this world, but we can't do it without remaining in him.

One way we show our love for Jesus is to do what he says is best for us. He knows this way of living won't be easy. That's why he tells us to remain in him every day . . . over and over and over. In Christ, the impossible becomes possible! When we remain in and with Christ, we are never alone. Always connected, we're never without hope. It's how we followers of Jesus are meant to live. ■

about me because you have been with me from the beginning of my ministry. ^{16:1}"I have told you these things so that you won't abandon your faith. ²For you will be expelled from the synagogues, and the time is coming when those who kill you will think they are doing a holy service for God. ³This is because they have never known the Father or me. ⁴Yes, I'm telling you these things now, so that when they happen, you will remember my warning. I didn't tell you earlier because I was going to be with you for a while longer.

The Work of the Holy Spirit

⁵"But now I am going away to the one who sent me, and not one of you is asking where I am going. ⁶Instead, you grieve because of what I've told you. ⁷But in fact, it is best for you that I go away, because if I don't, the Advocate won't come. If I do go away, then I will send him to you. ⁸And when he comes, he will convict the world of its sin, and of God's righteousness, and of the coming judgment. ⁹The world's sin is that it refuses to believe in me. ¹⁰Righteousness is available because I go to the Father, and you will see me no more. ¹¹Judgment will come because the ruler of this world has already been judged.

¹²"There is so much more I want to tell you, but you can't bear it now. ¹³When the Spirit of truth comes, he will guide you into all truth. He will not speak on his own but will tell you what he has heard. He will tell you about the future. ¹⁴He will bring me glory by telling you whatever he receives from me. ¹⁵All that belongs to the Father is mine;

Jesus is the champion. In any showdown between the messy world and Jesus, he wins. He wins for us—always.

this is why I said, 'The Spirit will tell you whatever he receives from me.'

Sadness Will Be Turned to Joy

¹⁶"In a little while you won't see me anymore. But a little while after that, you will see me again."

¹⁷Some of the disciples asked each other, "What does he mean when he says, 'In a little while you won't see me, but then you will see me,' and 'I am going to the Father'? ¹⁸And what does

he mean by 'a little while'? We don't understand."

[19] Jesus realized they wanted to ask him about it, so he said, "Are you asking yourselves what I meant? I said in a little while you won't see me, but a little while after that you will see me again. [20] I tell you the truth, you will weep and mourn over what is going to happen to me, but the world will rejoice. You will grieve, but your grief will suddenly turn to wonderful joy. [21] It will be like a woman suffering the pains of labor. When her child is born, her anguish gives way to joy because she has brought a new baby into the world. [22] So you have sorrow now, but I will see you again; then you will rejoice, and no one can rob you of that joy. [23] At that time you won't need to ask me for anything. I tell you the truth, you will ask the Father directly, and he will grant your request because you use my name. [24] You haven't done this before. Ask, using my name, and you will receive, and you will have abundant joy.

[25] "I have spoken of these matters in figures of speech, but soon I will stop speaking figuratively and will tell you plainly all about the Father. [26] Then you will ask in my name. I'm not saying I will ask the Father on your behalf, [27] for the Father himself loves you dearly because you love me and believe that I came from God. [28] Yes, I came from the Father into the world, and now I will leave the world and return to the Father."

[29] Then his disciples said, "At last you are speaking plainly and not figuratively. [30] Now we understand that you know everything, and there's no need to question you. From this we believe that you came from God."

[31] Jesus asked, "Do you finally believe? [32] But the time is coming—indeed it's here now—when you will be scattered, each one going his own way, leaving me alone. Yet I am not alone because the Father is with me. [33] I have told you all this so that you may have peace in me. Here on earth you will have many trials and sorrows. But take heart, because I have overcome the world."

Jesus Prays for His Followers

[17:1] After saying all these things, Jesus looked up to heaven and said, "Father, the hour has come. Glorify your Son so he can give glory back to you. [2] For you have given him authority over everyone. He gives eternal life to each one you have given him. [3] And this is the way to have eternal life—to know you, the only true God, and Jesus Christ, the one you sent to earth. [4] I brought glory to you here on earth by completing the work you gave me to do. [5] Now, Father, bring me into the glory we shared before the world began.

[6] "I have revealed you to the ones you gave me from this world. They were always yours. You gave them to me, and they have kept your word. [7] Now they know that everything I have is a gift from you, [8] for I have passed on to them the message you gave me. They accepted it and know that I came from you, and they believe you sent me.

[9] "My prayer is not for the world, but for those you have given me, because they belong to you. [10] All who are mine belong to you, and you have given them to me, so they bring me glory. [11] Now I

am departing from the world; they are staying in this world, but I am coming to you. Holy Father, you have given me your name; now protect them by the power of your name so that they will be united just as we are. ¹²During my time here, I protected them by the power of the name you gave me. I guarded them so that not one was lost, except the one headed for destruction, as the Scriptures foretold.

¹³"Now I am coming to you. I told them many things while I was with them in this world so they would be filled with my joy. ¹⁴I have given them your word. And the world hates them because they do not belong to the world, just as I do not belong to the world. ¹⁵I'm not asking you to take them out of the world, but to keep them safe from the evil one. ¹⁶They do not belong to this world any more than I do. ¹⁷Make them holy by your truth; teach them your word, which is truth. ¹⁸Just as you sent me into the world, I am sending them into the world. ¹⁹And I give myself as a holy sacrifice for them so they can be made holy by your truth.

²⁰"I am praying not only for these disciples but also for all who will ever believe in me through their message. ²¹I pray that they will all be one, just as you and I are one—as you are in me, Father, and I am in you. And may they be in us so that the world will believe you sent me.

²²"I have given them the glory you gave me, so they may be one as we are one. ²³I am in them and you are in me. May they experience such perfect unity that the world will know that you sent me and that you love them as much as you love me. ²⁴Father, I want these whom you have given me to be with me where I am. Then they can see all the glory you gave me because you loved me even before the world began!

²⁵"O righteous Father, the world doesn't know you, but I do; and these disciples know you sent me. ²⁶I have revealed you to them, and I will continue to do so. Then your love for me will be in them, and I will be in them."

Jesus Is Betrayed, Arrested, and Sentenced to Death

¹⁸:¹After saying these things, Jesus crossed the Kidron Valley with his disciples and entered a grove of olive trees. ²Judas, the betrayer, knew this place, because Jesus had often gone there with his disciples. ³The leading priests and Pharisees had given Judas a contingent of Roman soldiers and Temple guards to accompany him. Now with blazing torches, lanterns, and weapons, they arrived at the olive grove.

⁴Jesus fully realized all that was going to happen to him, so he stepped forward to meet them. "Who are you looking for?" he asked.

⁵"Jesus the Nazarene," they replied.

"I AM he," Jesus said. (Judas, who betrayed him, was standing with them.) ⁶As Jesus said "I AM he," they all drew back and fell to the ground! ⁷Once more he asked them, "Who are you looking for?"

And again they replied, "Jesus the Nazarene."

⁸"I told you that I AM he," Jesus said.

"And since I am the one you want, let these others go." [9]He did this to fulfill his own statement: "I did not lose a single one of those you have given me."

[10]Then Simon Peter drew a sword and slashed off the right ear of Malchus, the high priest's slave. [11]But Jesus said to Peter, "Put your sword back into its sheath. Shall I not drink from the cup of suffering the Father has given me?"

Jesus at the High Priest's House

[12]So the soldiers, their commanding officer, and the Temple guards arrested Jesus and tied him up. [13]First they took him to Annas, since he was the father-in-law of Caiaphas, the high priest at that time. [14]Caiaphas was the one who had told the other Jewish leaders, "It's better that one man should die for the people."

Peter's First Denial of Jesus

[15]Simon Peter followed Jesus, as did another of the disciples. That other disciple was acquainted with the high priest, so he was allowed to enter the high priest's courtyard with Jesus. [16]Pe-

"No," he said, "I am not."

[18]Because it was cold, the household servants and the guards had made a charcoal fire. They stood around it, warming themselves, and Peter stood with them, warming himself.

The High Priest Questions Jesus

[19]Inside, the high priest began asking Jesus about his followers and what he had been teaching them. [20]Jesus replied, "Everyone knows what I teach. I have preached regularly in the synagogues and the Temple, where the people gather. I have not spoken in secret. [21]Why are you asking me this question? Ask those who heard me. They know what I said."

[22]Then one of the Temple guards standing nearby slapped Jesus across the face. "Is that the way to answer the high priest?" he demanded.

[23]Jesus replied, "If I said anything wrong, you must prove it. But if I'm speaking the truth, why are you beating me?"

[24]Then Annas bound Jesus and sent him to Caiaphas, the high priest.

Jesus has an ongoing interest in us. It's amazing to think that he prayed for all of us (even in the present day) who have decided to follow him. How does his prayer for you affect you?

ter had to stay outside the gate. Then the disciple who knew the high priest spoke to the woman watching at the gate, and she let Peter in. [17]The woman asked Peter, "You're not one of that man's disciples, are you?"

Peter's Second and Third Denials

[25]Meanwhile, as Simon Peter was standing by the fire warming himself, they asked him again, "You're not one of his disciples, are you?"

He denied it, saying, "No, I am not."

²⁶But one of the household slaves of the high priest, a relative of the man whose ear Peter had cut off, asked, "Didn't I see you out there in the olive grove with Jesus?" ²⁷Again Peter denied it. And immediately a rooster crowed.

Jesus' Trial before Pilate

²⁸Jesus' trial before Caiaphas ended in the early hours of the morning. Then he was taken to the headquarters of the Roman governor. His accusers didn't go inside because it would defile them, and they wouldn't be allowed to celebrate the Passover. ²⁹So Pilate, the governor, went out to them and asked, "What is your charge against this man?"

³⁰"We wouldn't have handed him over to you if he weren't a criminal!" they retorted.

³¹"Then take him away and judge him by your own law," Pilate told them.

"Only the Romans are permitted to execute someone," the Jewish leaders replied. ³²(This fulfilled Jesus' prediction about the way he would die.)

³³Then Pilate went back into his headquarters and called for Jesus to be brought to him. "Are you the king of the Jews?" he asked him.

³⁴Jesus replied, "Is this your own question, or did others tell you about me?"

³⁵"Am I a Jew?" Pilate retorted. "Your own people and their leading priests brought you to me for trial. Why? What have you done?"

³⁶Jesus answered, "My Kingdom is not an earthly kingdom. If it were, my followers would fight to keep me from being handed over to the Jewish leaders. But my Kingdom is not of this world."

³⁷Pilate said, "So you are a king?"

Jesus responded, "You say I am a king. Actually, I was born and came into the world to testify to the truth. All who love the truth recognize that what I say is true."

³⁸"What is truth?" Pilate asked. Then he went out again to the people and told them, "He is not guilty of any crime. ³⁹But you have a custom of asking me to release one prisoner each year at Passover. Would you like me to release this 'King of the Jews'?"

⁴⁰But they shouted back, "No! Not this man. We want Barabbas!" (Barabbas was a revolutionary.)

Jesus Sentenced to Death

¹⁹:¹Then Pilate had Jesus flogged with a lead-tipped whip. ²The soldiers wove a crown of thorns and put it on his head, and they put a purple robe on him. ³"Hail! King of the Jews!" they mocked, as they slapped him across the face.

⁴Pilate went outside again and said to the people, "I am going to bring him out to you now, but understand clearly that I find him not guilty." ⁵Then Jesus came out wearing the crown of thorns and the purple robe. And Pilate said, "Look, here is the man!"

⁶When they saw him, the leading priests and Temple guards began shouting, "Crucify him! Crucify him!"

"Take him yourselves and crucify him," Pilate said. "I find him not guilty."

⁷The Jewish leaders replied, "By our law he ought to die because he called himself the Son of God."

⁸When Pilate heard this, he was

Jesus is willing to suffer for us.
He died on the cross, an excruciating execution, so that we can experience the love and life of God.

more frightened than ever. ⁹He took Jesus back into the headquarters again and asked him, "Where are you from?" But Jesus gave no answer. ¹⁰"Why don't you talk to me?" Pilate demanded. "Don't you realize that I have the power to release you or crucify you?"

¹¹Then Jesus said, "You would have no power over me at all unless it were given to you from above. So the one who handed me over to you has the greater sin."

¹²Then Pilate tried to release him, but the Jewish leaders shouted, "If you release this man, you are no 'friend of Caesar.' Anyone who declares himself a king is a rebel against Caesar."

¹³When they said this, Pilate brought Jesus out to them again. Then Pilate sat down on the judgment seat on the platform that is called the Stone Pavement (in Hebrew, *Gabbatha*). ¹⁴It was now about noon on the day of preparation for the Passover. And Pilate said to the people, "Look, here is your king!"

¹⁵"Away with him," they yelled. "Away with him! Crucify him!"

"What? Crucify your king?" Pilate asked.

"We have no king but Caesar," the leading priests shouted back.

¹⁶Then Pilate turned Jesus over to them to be crucified.

Jesus Dies, but Death Cannot Hold Him

So they took Jesus away. ¹⁷Carrying the cross by himself, he went to the place called Place of the Skull (in Hebrew, *Golgotha*). ¹⁸There they nailed him to the cross. Two others were crucified with him, one on either side, with Jesus between them. ¹⁹And Pilate posted a sign on the cross that read, "Jesus of Nazareth, the King of the Jews." ²⁰The place where Jesus was crucified was near the city, and the sign was written in Hebrew, Latin, and Greek, so that many people could read it.

²¹Then the leading priests objected and said to Pilate, "Change it from 'The King of the Jews' to 'He said, I am King of the Jews.'"

²²Pilate replied, "No, what I have written, I have written."

²³When the soldiers had crucified Jesus, they divided his clothes among the four of them. They also took his robe, but it was seamless, woven in one piece from top to bottom. ²⁴So they said, "Rather than tearing it apart, let's throw dice for it." This fulfilled the Scripture that says, "They divided my garments among themselves and threw dice for my clothing." So that is what they did.

²⁵Standing near the cross were Jesus' mother, and his mother's sister, Mary (the wife of Clopas), and Mary Magdalene. ²⁶When Jesus saw his mother standing there beside the disciple he loved, he said to her, "Dear woman, here is your son." ²⁷And he said to this disciple, "Here is your mother." And from then on this disciple took her into his home.

The Death of Jesus

²⁸Jesus knew that his mission was now finished, and to fulfill Scripture he said, "I am thirsty." ²⁹A jar of sour wine was sitting there, so they soaked a

sponge in it, put it on a hyssop branch, and held it up to his lips. ³⁰When Jesus had tasted it, he said, "It is finished!" Then he bowed his head and released his spirit.

³¹It was the day of preparation, and the Jewish leaders didn't want the bodies hanging there the next day, which was the Sabbath (and a very special Sabbath, because it was the Passover). So they asked Pilate to hasten their

³⁷and "They will look on the one they pierced."

The Burial of Jesus

³⁸Afterward Joseph of Arimathea, who had been a secret disciple of Jesus (because he feared the Jewish leaders), asked Pilate for permission to take down Jesus' body. When Pilate gave permission, Joseph came and took the body away. ³⁹With him came Nicode-

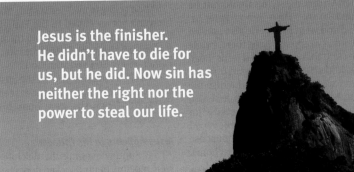

Jesus is the finisher. He didn't have to die for us, but he did. Now sin has neither the right nor the power to steal our life.

© CELSODINIZ/PHOTOS.COM

deaths by ordering that their legs be broken. Then their bodies could be taken down. ³²So the soldiers came and broke the legs of the two men crucified with Jesus. ³³But when they came to Jesus, they saw that he was already dead, so they didn't break his legs. ³⁴One of the soldiers, however, pierced his side with a spear, and immediately blood and water flowed out. ³⁵(This report is from an eyewitness giving an accurate account. He speaks the truth so that you also may continue to believe.) ³⁶These things happened in fulfillment of the Scriptures that say, "Not one of his bones will be broken,"

mus, the man who had come to Jesus at night. He brought about seventy-five pounds of perfumed ointment made from myrrh and aloes. ⁴⁰Following Jewish burial custom, they wrapped Jesus' body with the spices in long sheets of linen cloth. ⁴¹The place of crucifixion was near a garden, where there was a new tomb, never used before. ⁴²And so, because it was the day of preparation for the Jewish Passover and since the tomb was close at hand, they laid Jesus there.

The Resurrection

²⁰:¹Early on Sunday morning, while it was still dark, Mary Magdalene came to

the tomb and found that the stone had been rolled away from the entrance. [2]She ran and found Simon Peter and the other disciple, the one whom Jesus loved. She said, "They have taken the Lord's body out of the tomb, and we don't know where they have put him!"

[3]Peter and the other disciple started out for the tomb. [4]They were both running, but the other disciple outran Peter and reached the tomb first. [5]He stooped and looked in and saw the linen wrappings lying there, but he didn't go in. [6]Then Simon Peter arrived and went inside. He also noticed the linen wrappings lying there, [7]while the cloth that had covered Jesus' head was folded up and lying apart from the other wrappings. [8]Then the disciple who had reached the tomb first also went in, and he saw and believed—[9]for until then they still hadn't understood the Scriptures that said Jesus must rise from the dead. [10]Then they went home.

The Resurrected Jesus Shows He Is Alive

[11]Mary was standing outside the tomb crying, and as she wept, she stooped and looked in. [12]She saw two white-robed angels, one sitting at the head and the other at the foot of the place where the body of Jesus had been lying. [13]"Dear woman, why are you crying?" the angels asked her.

"Because they have taken away my Lord," she replied, "and I don't know where they have put him."

[14]She turned to leave and saw someone standing there. It was Jesus, but she didn't recognize him. [15]"Dear woman, why are you crying?" Jesus asked her. "Who are you looking for?"

She thought he was the gardener. "Sir," she said, "if you have taken him away, tell me where you have put him, and I will go and get him."

[16]"Mary!" Jesus said.

She turned to him and cried out, "Rabboni!" (which is Hebrew for "Teacher").

[17]"Don't cling to me," Jesus said, "for I haven't yet ascended to the Father. But go find my brothers and tell them, 'I am ascending to my Father and your Father, to my God and your God.'"

[18]Mary Magdalene found the disciples and told them, "I have seen the Lord!" Then she gave them his message.

Jesus Appears to His Followers

[19]That Sunday evening the disciples were meeting behind locked doors because they were afraid of the Jewish leaders. Suddenly, Jesus was standing there among them! "Peace be with you," he said. [20]As he spoke, he showed them the wounds in his hands and his side. They were filled with joy when they saw the Lord! [21]Again he said, "Peace be with you. As the Father has sent me, so I am sending you." [22]Then he breathed on them and said, "Receive the Holy Spirit. [23]If you forgive anyone's sins, they are forgiven. If you do not forgive them, they are not forgiven."

Jesus Appears to Thomas

[24]One of the twelve disciples, Thomas (nicknamed the Twin), was not with

the others when Jesus came. [25]They told him, "We have seen the Lord!"

But he replied, "I won't believe it unless I see the nail wounds in his hands, put my fingers into them, and place my hand into the wound in his side."

[26]Eight days later the disciples were together again, and this time Thomas was with them. The doors were locked; but suddenly, as before, Jesus was standing among them. "Peace be with you," he said. [27]Then he said to

the disciples were there—Simon Peter, Thomas (nicknamed the Twin), Nathanael from Cana in Galilee, the sons of Zebedee, and two other disciples.

[3]Simon Peter said, "I'm going fishing."

"We'll come, too," they all said. So they went out in the boat, but they caught nothing all night.

[4]At dawn Jesus was standing on the beach, but the disciples couldn't see who he was. [5]He called out, "Fellows,

---

Faith means that believing is seeing. By faith we take up work assignments that continue Jesus' mission. What do you still need to help you move onto Jesus' mission team?

Thomas, "Put your finger here, and look at my hands. Put your hand into the wound in my side. Don't be faithless any longer. Believe!"

[28]"My Lord and my God!" Thomas exclaimed.

[29]Then Jesus told him, "You believe because you have seen me. Blessed are those who believe without seeing me."

Why John Wrote This Book

[30]The disciples saw Jesus do many other miraculous signs in addition to the ones recorded in this book. [31]But these are written so that you may continue to believe that Jesus is the Messiah, the Son of God, and that by believing in him you will have life by the power of his name.

Jesus Appears to Seven Disciples

[21:1]Later, Jesus appeared again to the disciples beside the Sea of Galilee. This is how it happened. [2]Several of

have you caught any fish?"

"No," they replied.

[6]Then he said, "Throw out your net on the right-hand side of the boat, and you'll get some!" So they did, and they couldn't haul in the net because there were so many fish in it.

[7]Then the disciple Jesus loved said to Peter, "It's the Lord!" When Simon Peter heard that it was the Lord, he put on his tunic (for he had stripped for work), jumped into the water, and headed to shore. [8]The others stayed with the boat and pulled the loaded net to the shore, for they were only about a hundred yards from shore. [9]When they got there, they found breakfast waiting for them—fish cooking over a charcoal fire, and some bread.

[10]"Bring some of the fish you've just caught," Jesus said. [11]So Simon Peter went aboard and dragged the net to the

/// continued on page 67

Jesus is alive. Now.
The historical fact of
Jesus' resurrection from
the dead is the one truth
that changes absolutely
everything.

Unrecognized, Jesus Walks with Two Followers

T HAT SAME DAY two of Jesus' followers were walking to the village of Emmaus, seven miles from Jerusalem. [14]As they walked along they were talking about everything that had happened. [15] As they talked and discussed these things, Jesus himself suddenly came and began walking with them. [16]But God kept them from recognizing him.

[17]He asked them, "What are you discussing so intently as you walk along?"

They stopped short, sadness written across their faces. [18]Then one of them, Cleopas, replied, "You must be the only person in Jerusalem who hasn't heard about all the things that have happened there the last few days."

[19]"What things?" Jesus asked.

"The things that happened to Jesus, the man from Nazareth," they said. "He was a prophet who did powerful miracles, and he was a mighty teacher in the eyes of God and all the people. [20]But our leading priests and other religious leaders handed him over to be condemned to death, and they crucified him. [21]We had hoped he was the Messiah who had come to rescue Israel. This all happened three days ago.

[22]"Then some women from our group of his followers were at his tomb early this morning, and they came back with an amazing report. [23]They said his body was missing, and they had seen angels who told them Jesus is alive! [24]Some of our men ran out to see, and sure enough, his body was gone, just as the women had said."

[25]Then Jesus said to them, "You foolish people! You find it so hard to believe all that the prophets wrote in the Scriptures. [26]Wasn't it clearly predicted that the Messiah would have to suffer all these things before entering his glory?" [27]Then Jesus took them through

Jesus is the most amazing travel companion we could ever imagine. Wherever we're going, whatever our mood, he makes our journey epic.

the writings of Moses and all the prophets, explaining from all the Scriptures the things concerning himself.

[28]By this time they were nearing Emmaus and the end of their journey. Jesus acted as if he were going on, [29]but they begged him, "Stay the night with us, since it is getting late." So he went home with them. [30]As they sat down to eat, he took the bread and blessed it. Then he broke it and gave it to them. [31]Suddenly, their eyes were opened, and they recognized him. And at that moment he disappeared!

[32]They said to each other, "Didn't our hearts burn within us as he talked with us on the road and explained the Scriptures to us?" [33]And within the hour they were on their way back to Jerusalem. There they found the eleven disciples and the others who had gathered with them, [34]who said, "The Lord has really risen! He appeared to Peter."

Jesus Appears to Many Followers

³⁵ Then the two from Emmaus told their story of how Jesus had appeared to them as they were walking along the road, and how they had recognized him as he was breaking the bread. ³⁶ And just as they were telling about it, Jesus himself was suddenly standing there among them. "Peace be with you," he said. ³⁷ But the whole group was startled and frightened, thinking they were seeing a ghost!

³⁸ "Why are you frightened?" he asked. "Why are your hearts filled with doubt? ³⁹ Look at my hands. Look at my feet. You can see that it's really me. Touch me and make sure that I am not a ghost, because ghosts don't have bodies, as you see that I do." ⁴⁰ As he spoke, he showed them his hands and his feet.

⁴¹ Still they stood there in disbelief, filled with joy and wonder. Then he asked them, "Do you have anything here to eat?" ⁴² They gave him a piece of broiled fish, ⁴³ and he ate it as they watched.

⁴⁴ Then he said, "When I was with you before, I told you that everything written about me in the law of Moses and the prophets and in the Psalms must be fulfilled." ⁴⁵ Then he opened their minds to understand the Scriptures. ⁴⁶ And he said, "Yes, it was written long ago that the Messiah would suffer and die and rise from the dead on the third day. ⁴⁷ It was also written that this message would be proclaimed in the authority of his name to all the nations, beginning in Jerusalem: 'There is forgiveness of sins for all who repent.' ⁴⁸ You are witnesses of all these things.

⁴⁹ "And now I will send the Holy Spirit, just as my Father promised. But stay here in the city until the Holy Spirit comes and fills you with power from heaven." ■

/// *continued from page 61*

shore. There were 153 large fish, and yet the net hadn't torn.

¹²"Now come and have some breakfast!" Jesus said. None of the disciples dared to ask him, "Who are you?" They knew it was the Lord. ¹³Then Jesus served them the bread and the fish. ¹⁴This was the third time Jesus had appeared to his disciples since he had been raised from the dead.

¹⁵After breakfast Jesus asked Simon Peter, "Simon son of John, do you love me more than these?"

"Yes, Lord," Peter replied, "you know I love you."

were young, you were able to do as you liked; you dressed yourself and went wherever you wanted to go. But when you are old, you will stretch out your hands, and others will dress you and take you where you don't want to go." ¹⁹Jesus said this to let him know by what kind of death he would glorify God. Then Jesus told him, "Follow me."

²⁰Peter turned around and saw behind them the disciple Jesus loved—the one who had leaned over to Jesus during supper and asked, "Lord, who will betray you?" ²¹Peter asked Jesus, "What about him, Lord?"

²²Jesus replied, "If I want him to re-

> Don't let past failures paralyze you. Neither should you let other's journeys distract you. What do you think Jesus would say to you about what holds you back?

"Then feed my lambs," Jesus told him.

¹⁶Jesus repeated the question: "Simon son of John, do you love me?"

"Yes, Lord," Peter said, "you know I love you."

"Then take care of my sheep," Jesus said.

¹⁷A third time he asked him, "Simon son of John, do you love me?"

Peter was hurt that Jesus asked the question a third time. He said, "Lord, you know everything. You know that I love you."

Jesus said, "Then feed my sheep. ¹⁸"I tell you the truth, when you

main alive until I return, what is that to you? As for you, follow me." ²³So the rumor spread among the community of believers that this disciple wouldn't die. But that isn't what Jesus said at all. He only said, "If I want him to remain alive until I return, what is that to you?"

²⁴This disciple is the one who testifies to these events and has recorded them here. And we know that his account of these things is accurate.

²⁵Jesus also did many other things. If they were all written down, I suppose the whole world could not contain the books that would be written.

THE BOOK OF ACTS

One of the Gospel writers, Luke, also wrote a sequel to the life and times of Jesus. It's the story of how Jesus continued his activity on earth by working through his followers by the power of the Holy Spirit. Here are the first eleven chapters of the book of Acts. If you want to read the rest, grab a Bible and pick up where you left off.

Jesus Prepares His Followers to Continue His Work

1:1 In my first book I told you, Theophilus, about everything Jesus began to do and teach 2 until the day he was taken up to heaven after giving his chosen apostles further instructions through the Holy Spirit. 3 During the forty days after he suffered and died, he appeared to the apostles from time to time, and he proved to them in many ways that he was actually alive. And he talked to them about the Kingdom of God.

4 Once when he was eating with them, he commanded them, "Do not leave Jerusalem until the Father sends you the gift he promised, as I told you before. 5 John baptized with water, but in just a few days you will be baptized with the Holy Spirit."

Jesus Ascends to Heaven

6 So when the apostles were with Jesus, they kept asking him, "Lord, has the time come for you to free Israel and restore our kingdom?"

7 He replied, "The Father alone has the authority to set those dates and times, and they are not for you to know.

8 But you will receive power when the Holy Spirit comes upon you. And you will be my witnesses, telling people about me everywhere—in Jerusalem, throughout Judea, in Samaria, and to the ends of the earth."

9 After saying this, he was taken up into a cloud while they were watching, and they could no longer see him. 10 As they strained to see him rising into heaven, two white-robed men suddenly stood among them. 11 "Men of Galilee," they said, "why are you standing here staring into heaven? Jesus has been taken from you into heaven, but someday he will return from heaven in the same way you saw him go!"

Matthias Replaces Judas

12 Then the apostles returned to Jerusalem from the Mount of Olives, a distance of half a mile. 13 When they arrived, they went to the upstairs room of the house where they were staying.

Here are the names of those who were present: Peter, John, James, Andrew, Philip, Thomas, Bartholomew, Matthew, James (son of Alphaeus), Simon (the Zealot), and Judas (son of James). 14 They all met together and were constantly united in prayer, along with Mary the mother of Jesus, several other women, and the brothers of Jesus.

15 During this time, when about 120 believers were together in one place, Peter stood up and addressed them. 16 "Brothers," he said, "the Scriptures had to be fulfilled concerning Judas, who guided those who arrested Jesus. This was predicted long ago by the Holy Spirit, speaking through King David. 17 Judas was one of us and shared in the ministry with us."

18 (Judas had bought a field with the money he received for his treachery. Falling headfirst there, his body split open, spilling out all his intestines. 19 The news of his death spread to all the people of Jerusalem, and they gave the place the Aramaic name *Akeldama,* which means "Field of Blood.")

20 Peter continued, "This was written in the book of Psalms, where it says, 'Let his home become desolate, with no one living in it.' It also says, 'Let someone else take his position.'

21 "So now we must choose a replacement for Judas from among the men who were with us the entire time we were traveling with the Lord Jesus—22 from the time he was baptized by John until the day he was taken from us. Whoever is chosen will join us as a witness of Jesus' resurrection."

23 So they nominated two men: Joseph called Barsabbas (also known as Justus) and Matthias. 24 Then they all prayed, "O Lord, you know every heart. Show us which of these men you have chosen 25 as an apostle to replace Judas in this ministry, for he has deserted us and gone where he belongs." 26 Then they cast lots, and Matthias was selected to become an apostle with the other eleven.

Ordinary People Given God's Power

2 1 On the day of Pentecost all the believers were meeting together in one place. 2 Suddenly, there was a sound from heaven like the roaring of a mighty windstorm, and it filled the house where they were sitting. 3 Then, what looked like flames or tongues of fire appeared and settled on each of them. 4 And everyone present was filled with the Holy Spirit and began speaking in other languages, as the Holy Spirit gave them this ability.

5 At that time there were devout Jews from every nation living in Jerusalem. 6 When they heard the loud noise, everyone came running, and they were bewildered to hear their own languages being spoken by the believers. 7 They were completely amazed. "How can this be?" they exclaimed. "These people are all from Galilee,

Jesus is not retired. He still actively directs his followers into the life that he wants us to have.

and yet we hear them speaking in our own native languages! ⁹Here we are—Parthians, Medes, Elamites, people from Mesopotamia, Judea, Cappadocia, Pontus, the province of Asia, ¹⁰Phrygia, Pamphylia, Egypt, and the areas of Libya around Cyrene, visitors from Rome ¹¹(both Jews and converts to Judaism), Cretans, and Arabs. And we all hear these people speaking in our own languages about the wonderful things God has done!" ¹²They stood there amazed and perplexed. "What can this mean?" they asked each other.

¹³But others in the crowd ridiculed them, saying, "They're just drunk, that's all!"

Your young men will see visions,
    and your old men will dream
    dreams.
¹⁸ In those days I will pour out my
    Spirit
    even on my servants—men and
    women alike—
    and they will prophesy.
¹⁹ And I will cause wonders in the
    heavens above
    and signs on the earth below—
    blood and fire and clouds of
    smoke.
²⁰ The sun will become dark,
    and the moon will turn blood
    red
    before that great and glorious

Sometimes our biggest problem is that we don't think we should have to wait on anything. If you were convinced that Jesus would come through for you, how long would you be willing to wait?

Peter Preaches to the Crowd

¹⁴Then Peter stepped forward with the eleven other apostles and shouted to the crowd, "Listen carefully, all of you, fellow Jews and residents of Jerusalem! Make no mistake about this. ¹⁵These people are not drunk, as some of you are assuming. Nine o'clock in the morning is much too early for that. ¹⁶No, what you see was predicted long ago by the prophet Joel:

¹⁷ 'In the last days,' God says,
    'I will pour out my Spirit upon
    all people.
    Your sons and daughters will
    prophesy.

day of the Lord arrives.
²¹ But everyone who calls on the
    name of the Lord
    will be saved.'

²²"People of Israel, listen! God publicly endorsed Jesus the Nazarene by doing powerful miracles, wonders, and signs through him, as you well know. ²³But God knew what would happen, and his prearranged plan was carried out when Jesus was betrayed. With the help of lawless Gentiles, you nailed him to a cross and killed him. ²⁴But God released him from the horrors of death and raised him back to life, for death could not keep him in its grip. ²⁵King David said this about him:

'I see that the LORD is always with
me.
I will not be shaken, for he is
right beside me.
26 No wonder my heart is glad,
and my tongue shouts his
praises!
My body rests in hope.
27 For you will not leave my soul
among the dead
or allow your Holy One to rot in
the grave.
28 You have shown me the way of life,
and you will fill me with the joy
of your presence.'

29 "Dear brothers, think about this!
You can be sure that the patriarch David
wasn't referring to himself, for he
died and was buried, and his tomb
is still here among us. 30 But he was a
prophet, and he knew God had promised
with an oath that one of David's
own descendants would sit on his
throne. 31 David was looking into the
future and speaking of the Messiah's
resurrection. He was saying that God
would not leave him among the dead
or allow his body to rot in the grave.

32 "God raised Jesus from the dead,
and we are all witnesses of this. 33 Now
he is exalted to the place of highest
honor in heaven, at God's right hand.
And the Father, as he had promised,
gave him the Holy Spirit to pour out
upon us, just as you see and hear today.
34 For David himself never ascended
into heaven, yet he said,

'The LORD said to my Lord,
"Sit in the place of honor at my
right hand
35 until I humble your enemies,

making them a footstool under
your feet."'

36 "So let everyone in Israel know for
certain that God has made this Jesus,
whom you crucified, to be both Lord
and Messiah!"

37 Peter's words pierced their hearts,
and they said to him and to the other
apostles, "Brothers, what should we
do?"

38 Peter replied, "Each of you must repent
of your sins and turn to God, and
be baptized in the name of Jesus Christ
for the forgiveness of your sins. Then
you will receive the gift of the Holy
Spirit. 39 This promise is to you, to your
children, and to those far away—all
who have been called by the Lord our
God." 40 Then Peter continued preaching
for a long time, strongly urging all
his listeners, "Save yourselves from
this crooked generation!"

41 Those who believed what Peter
said were baptized and added to the
church that day—about 3,000 in all.

The Believers Form a Community

42 All the believers devoted themselves
to the apostles' teaching, and to fellowship,
and to sharing in meals (including
the Lord's Supper), and to prayer.

43 A deep sense of awe came over
them all, and the apostles performed
many miraculous signs and wonders.
44 And all the believers met together in
one place and shared everything they
had. 45 They sold their property and
possessions and shared the money
with those in need. 46 They worshiped
together at the Temple each day, met
in homes for the Lord's Supper, and
shared their meals with great joy and
generosity—47 all the while praising

God and enjoying the goodwill of all the people. And each day the Lord added to their fellowship those who were being saved.

Jesus' Followers Share His Love and Power

3 [1] Peter and John went to the Temple one afternoon to take part in the three o'clock prayer service. [2] As they approached the Temple, a man lame from birth was being carried in. Each day he was put beside the Temple gate, the one called the Beautiful Gate, so he could beg from the people going into the Temple. [3] When he saw Peter and John about to enter, he asked them for some money.

[4] Peter and John looked at him intently, and Peter said, "Look at us!" [5] The lame man looked at them eagerly, expecting some money. [6] But Peter said, "I don't have any silver or gold for you. But I'll give you what I have. In the name of Jesus Christ the Nazarene, get up and walk!"

[7] Then Peter took the lame man by the right hand and helped him up. And as he did, the man's feet and ankles were instantly healed and strengthened. [8] He jumped up, stood on his feet, and began to walk! Then, walking, leaping, and praising God, he went into the Temple with them.

[9] All the people saw him walking and heard him praising God. [10] When they realized he was the lame beggar they had seen so often at the Beautiful Gate, they were absolutely astounded!

[11] They all rushed out in amazement to Solomon's Colonnade, where the man was holding tightly to Peter and John.

Peter Preaches in the Temple

[12] Peter saw his opportunity and addressed the crowd. "People of Israel," he said, "what is so surprising about this? And why stare at us as though we had made this man walk by our own power or godliness? [13] For it is the God of Abraham, Isaac, and Jacob—the God of all our ancestors—who has brought glory to his servant Jesus by doing this. This is the same Jesus whom you handed over and rejected before Pilate, despite Pilate's decision to release him. [14] You rejected this holy, righteous one and instead demanded the release of a murderer. [15] You killed the author of life, but God raised him from the dead. And we are witnesses of this fact!

[16] "Through faith in the name of Jesus, this man was healed—and you know how crippled he was before. Faith in Jesus' name has healed him before your very eyes.

[17] "Friends, I realize that what you and your leaders did to Jesus was done in ignorance. [18] But God was fulfilling what all the prophets had foretold about the Messiah—that he must suffer these things. [19] Now repent of your sins and turn to God, so that your sins may be wiped away. [20] Then times of refreshment will come from the presence of the Lord, and he will again send you Jesus, your appointed Messiah. [21] For he must remain in heaven until the time for the final restoration of all things, as God promised long ago through his holy prophets. [22] Moses said, 'The LORD your God will raise up for you a Prophet

like me from among your own people. Listen carefully to everything he tells you.' ²³Then Moses said, 'Anyone who will not listen to that Prophet will be completely cut off from God's people.'

²⁴"Starting with Samuel, every prophet spoke about what is happening today. ²⁵You are the children of those prophets, and you are included in the covenant God promised to your ancestors. For God said to Abraham, 'Through your descendants all the families on earth will be blessed.' ²⁶When God raised up his servant, Jesus, he sent him first to you people of Israel, to bless you by turning each of you back from your sinful ways."

Peter and John before the Religious Leaders

4:1While Peter and John were speaking to the people, they were confronted by the priests, the captain of the Temple guard, and some of the Sadducees. ²These leaders were very disturbed that Peter and John were teaching the people that through Jesus there is a resurrection of the dead. ³They arrested them and, since it was already evening, put them in jail until morning. ⁴But many of the people who heard their message believed it, so the number of believers now totaled about 5,000 men, not counting women and children.

⁵The next day the council of all the rulers and elders and teachers of religious law met in Jerusalem. ⁶Annas the high priest was there, along with Caiaphas, John, Alexander, and other relatives of the high priest. ⁷They brought in the two disciples and demanded, "By what power, or in whose name, have you done this?"

⁸Then Peter, filled with the Holy Spirit, said to them, "Rulers and elders of our people, ⁹are we being questioned today because we've done a good deed for a crippled man? Do you want to know how he was healed? ¹⁰Let me clearly state to all of you and to all

Jesus is the name, the presence, the power, and the hope through which his followers change their world in amazing ways.

the people of Israel that he was healed by the powerful name of Jesus Christ the Nazarene, the man you crucified but whom God raised from the dead. ¹¹For Jesus is the one referred to in the Scriptures, where it says,

'The stone that you builders rejected
    has now become the cornerstone.'

¹²There is salvation in no one else! God has given no other name under heaven by which we must be saved."

¹³The members of the council were amazed when they saw the boldness of Peter and John, for they could see that they were ordinary men with no special training in the Scriptures. They also recognized them as men who had been with Jesus. ¹⁴But since they could see the man who had been healed standing right there among them, there was nothing the council could say. ¹⁵So they ordered Peter and John out of the council chamber and conferred among themselves.

¹⁶"What should we do with these men?" they asked each other. "We can't deny that they have performed a miraculous sign, and everybody in Jerusalem knows about it. ¹⁷But to keep them from spreading their propaganda any further, we must warn them not to speak to anyone in Jesus' name again."

¹⁸So they called the apostles back in and commanded them never again to speak or teach in the name of Jesus.

¹⁹But Peter and John replied, "Do you think God wants us to obey you rather than him? ²⁰We cannot stop telling about everything we have seen and heard."

²¹The council then threatened them further, but they finally let them go because they didn't know how to punish them without starting a riot. For everyone was praising God ²²for this miraculous sign—the healing of a man who had been lame for more than forty years.

The Believers Pray for Courage

²³As soon as they were freed, Peter and John returned to the other believers and told them what the leading priests and elders had said. ²⁴When they heard the report, all the believers lifted their voices together in prayer to God: "O Sovereign Lord, Creator of heaven and earth, the sea, and everything in them—²⁵you spoke long ago by the Holy Spirit through our ancestor David, your servant, saying,

'Why were the nations so angry?
    Why did they waste their time
        with futile plans?
²⁶ The kings of the earth prepared for battle;
    the rulers gathered together

Fear keeps a lot of people from making big life changes. But when Jesus came back to life, his followers overcame fears that once paralyzed them. What fears are you stuck in?

Jesus is large and in charge—still and always. Headlines, laws, armies, economies, enemies, bosses . . . none of them rule. Jesus does.

against the LORD
    and against his Messiah.'

²⁷"In fact, this has happened here in this very city! For Herod Antipas, Pontius Pilate the governor, the Gentiles, and the people of Israel were all united against Jesus, your holy servant, whom you anointed. ²⁸But everything they did was determined beforehand according to your will. ²⁹And now, O Lord, hear their threats, and give us, your servants, great boldness in preaching your word. ³⁰Stretch out your hand with healing power; may miraculous signs and wonders be done through the name of your holy servant Jesus."

³¹After this prayer, the meeting place shook, and they were all filled with the Holy Spirit. Then they preached the word of God with boldness.

The Believers Share Their Possessions

³²All the believers were united in heart and mind. And they felt that what they owned was not their own, so they shared everything they had. ³³The apostles testified powerfully to the resurrection of the Lord Jesus, and God's great blessing was upon them all. ³⁴There were no needy people among them, because those who owned land or houses would sell them ³⁵and bring the money to the apostles to give to those in need.

³⁶For instance, there was Joseph, the one the apostles nicknamed Barnabas (which means "Son of Encouragement"). He was from the tribe of Levi and came from the island of Cyprus. ³⁷He sold a field he owned and brought the money to the apostles.

Ananias and Sapphira

5:1 But there was a certain man named Ananias who, with his wife, Sapphira, sold some property. ²He brought part of the money to the apostles, claiming it was the full amount. With his wife's consent, he kept the rest.

³Then Peter said, "Ananias, why have you let Satan fill your heart? You lied to the Holy Spirit, and you kept some of the money for yourself. ⁴The property was yours to sell or not sell, as you wished. And after selling it, the money was also yours to give away. How could you do a thing like this? You weren't lying to us but to God!"

⁵As soon as Ananias heard these words, he fell to the floor and died. Everyone who heard about it was terrified. ⁶Then some young men got up, wrapped him in a sheet, and took him out and buried him.

⁷About three hours later his wife came in, not knowing what had happened. ⁸Peter asked her, "Was this the price you and your husband received for your land?"

"Yes," she replied, "that was the price."

⁹And Peter said, "How could the two of you even think of conspiring to test the Spirit of the Lord like this? The young men who buried your husband are just outside the door, and they will carry you out, too."

¹⁰Instantly, she fell to the floor and died. When the young men came in and saw that she was dead, they carried her out and buried her beside her husband. ¹¹Great fear gripped the entire church and everyone else who heard what had happened.

The Apostles Heal Many People

¹²The apostles were performing many miraculous signs and wonders among the people. And all the believers were meeting regularly at the Temple in the area known as Solomon's Colonnade. ¹³But no one else dared to join them,

even though all the people had high regard for them. ¹⁴Yet more and more people believed and were brought to the Lord—crowds of both men and women. ¹⁵As a result of the apostles' work, sick people were brought out into the streets on beds and mats so that Peter's shadow might fall across some of them as he went by. ¹⁶Crowds came from the villages around Jerusalem, bringing their sick and those possessed by evil spirits, and they were all healed.

Jesus' Followers Face Stiff Opposition

¹⁷The high priest and his officials, who were Sadducees, were filled with jealousy. ¹⁸They arrested the apostles and put them in the public jail. ¹⁹But an angel of the Lord came at night, opened the gates of the jail, and brought them out. Then he told them, ²⁰"Go to the Temple and give the people this message of life!"

²¹So at daybreak the apostles entered the Temple, as they were told, and immediately began teaching.

When the high priest and his officials arrived, they convened the high council—the full assembly of the elders of Israel. Then they sent for the apostles to be brought from the jail for trial. ²²But when the Temple guards went to the jail, the men were gone. So they returned to the council and reported, ²³"The jail was securely locked, with the guards standing outside, but when we opened the gates, no one was there!"

²⁴When the captain of the Temple guard and the leading priests heard this, they were perplexed, wondering where it would all end. ²⁵Then someone arrived with startling news: "The men you put in jail are standing in the Temple, teaching the people!"

²⁶The captain went with his Temple guards and arrested the apostles, but without violence, for they were afraid the people would stone them. ²⁷Then they brought the apostles before the high council, where the high priest confronted them. ²⁸"We gave you strict orders never again to teach in this man's name!" he said. "Instead, you have filled all Jerusalem with your teaching about him, and you want to make us responsible for his death!"

²⁹But Peter and the apostles replied, "We must obey God rather than any human authority. ³⁰The God of our ancestors raised Jesus from the dead after you killed him by hanging him on a cross. ³¹Then God put him in the place of honor at his right hand as Prince and Savior. He did this so the people of Israel would repent of their sins and be forgiven. ³²We are witnesses of these things and so is the Holy Spirit, who is given by God to those who obey him."

³³When they heard this, the high council was furious and decided to kill them. ³⁴But one member, a Pharisee named Gamaliel, who was an expert in religious law and respected by all the people, stood up and ordered that the men be sent outside the council chamber for a while. ³⁵Then he said to his colleagues, "Men of Israel, take care what you are planning to do to these men! ³⁶Some time ago there was that fellow Theudas, who pretended to be someone great. About 400 others joined him, but he was killed, and all his followers went their various ways. The whole movement came to nothing. ³⁷After him, at the time of the census, there was Judas of Galilee. He got people to follow him, but he was killed, too, and all his followers were scattered.

³⁸"So my advice is, leave these men alone. Let them go. If they are planning and doing these things merely on their own, it will soon be overthrown. ³⁹But if it is from God, you will not be able to overthrow them. You may even find yourselves fighting against God!"

⁴⁰The others accepted his advice. They called in the apostles and had them flogged. Then they ordered them never again to speak in the name of Jesus, and they let them go.

⁴¹The apostles left the high council rejoicing that God had counted them worthy to suffer disgrace for the name of Jesus. ⁴²And every day, in the Temple and from house to house, they continued to teach and preach this message: "Jesus is the Messiah."

Seven Servants Appointed to Help

⁶:¹But as the believers rapidly multiplied, there were rumblings of discontent. The Greek-speaking believers complained about the Hebrew-speaking believers, saying that their widows were being discriminated against in the daily distribution of food.

²So the Twelve called a meeting of all the believers. They said, "We apostles should spend our time teaching the word of God, not running a food program. ³And so, brothers, select seven men who are well respected and are

full of the Spirit and wisdom. We will give them this responsibility. ⁴Then we apostles can spend our time in prayer and teaching the word."

⁵Everyone liked this idea, and they chose the following: Stephen (a man full of faith and the Holy Spirit), Philip, Procorus, Nicanor, Timon, Parmenas, and Nicolas of Antioch (an earlier convert to the Jewish faith). ⁶These seven were presented to the apostles, who prayed for them as they laid their hands on them.

⁷So God's message continued to spread. The number of believers greatly increased in Jerusalem, and many of the Jewish priests were converted, too.

Stephen Is Arrested

⁸Stephen, a man full of God's grace and power, performed amazing miracles and signs among the people. ⁹But one day some men from the Synagogue of Freed Slaves, as it was called, started to debate with him. They were Jews from Cyrene, Alexandria, Cilicia, and the province of Asia. ¹⁰None of them could stand against the wisdom and the Spirit with which Stephen spoke.

¹¹So they persuaded some men to lie about Stephen, saying, "We heard him blaspheme Moses, and even God." ¹²This roused the people, the elders, and the teachers of religious law. So they arrested Stephen and brought him before the high council.

¹³The lying witnesses said, "This man is always speaking against the holy Temple and against the law of Moses. ¹⁴We have heard him say that this Jesus of Nazareth will destroy the Temple and change the customs Moses handed down to us."

¹⁵At this point everyone in the high council stared at Stephen, because his face became as bright as an angel's.

Stephen Addresses the Religious Leaders

⁷:¹Then the high priest asked Stephen, "Are these accusations true?"

²This was Stephen's reply: "Brothers and fathers, listen to me. Our glorious God appeared to our ancestor Abraham in Mesopotamia before he settled in Haran. ³God told him, 'Leave your native land and your relatives, and come into the land that I will show you.' ⁴So Abraham left the land of the Chaldeans and lived in Haran until his father died. Then God brought him here to the land where you now live.

⁵"But God gave him no inheritance here, not even one square foot of land. God did promise, however, that eventually the whole land would belong to Abraham and his descendants—even though he had no children yet. ⁶God also told him that his descendants would live in a foreign land, where they would be oppressed as slaves for 400 years. ⁷'But I will punish the nation that enslaves them,' God said, 'and in the end they will come out and worship me here in this place.'

⁸"God also gave Abraham the covenant of circumcision at that time. So when Abraham became the father of Isaac, he circumcised him on the eighth day. And the practice was continued when Isaac became the father of Jacob, and when Jacob became the father of the twelve patriarchs of the Israelite nation.

⁹"These patriarchs were jealous of their brother Joseph, and they sold

him to be a slave in Egypt. But God was with him [10]and rescued him from all his troubles. And God gave him favor before Pharaoh, king of Egypt. God also gave Joseph unusual wisdom, so that Pharaoh appointed him governor over all of Egypt and put him in charge of the palace.

[11]"But a famine came upon Egypt and Canaan. There was great misery, and our ancestors ran out of food. [12]Jacob heard that there was still grain in Egypt, so he sent his sons—our ancestors—to buy some. [13]The second time they went, Joseph revealed his identity to his brothers, and they were introduced to Pharaoh. [14]Then Joseph sent for his father, Jacob, and all his relatives to come to Egypt, seventy-five persons in all. [15]So Jacob went to Egypt. He died there, as did our ancestors.

beautiful child in God's eyes. His parents cared for him at home for three months. [21]When they had to abandon him, Pharaoh's daughter adopted him and raised him as her own son. [22]Moses was taught all the wisdom of the Egyptians, and he was powerful in both speech and action.

[23]"One day when Moses was forty years old, he decided to visit his relatives, the people of Israel. [24]He saw an Egyptian mistreating an Israelite. So Moses came to the man's defense and avenged him, killing the Egyptian. [25]Moses assumed his fellow Israelites would realize that God had sent him to rescue them, but they didn't.

[26]"The next day he visited them again and saw two men of Israel fighting. He tried to be a peacemaker. 'Men,' he said, 'you are brothers. Why are you

The word gets out when we do good deeds. Are you willing to be identified with Jesus by serving others selflessly, as he did?

[16]Their bodies were taken to Shechem and buried in the tomb Abraham had bought for a certain price from Hamor's sons in Shechem.

[17]"As the time drew near when God would fulfill his promise to Abraham, the number of our people in Egypt greatly increased. [18]But then a new king came to the throne of Egypt who knew nothing about Joseph. [19]This king exploited our people and oppressed them, forcing parents to abandon their newborn babies so they would die.

[20]"At that time Moses was born—a

fighting each other?'

[27]"But the man in the wrong pushed Moses aside. 'Who made you a ruler and judge over us?' he asked. [28]'Are you going to kill me as you killed that Egyptian yesterday?' [29]When Moses heard that, he fled the country and lived as a foreigner in the land of Midian. There his two sons were born.

[30]"Forty years later, in the desert near Mount Sinai, an angel appeared to Moses in the flame of a burning bush. [31]When Moses saw it, he was amazed at the sight. As he went to take a closer

look, the voice of the LORD called out to him, 32 'I am the God of your ancestors—the God of Abraham, Isaac, and Jacob.' Moses shook with terror and did not dare to look.

33 "Then the LORD said to him, 'Take off your sandals, for you are standing on holy ground. 34 I have certainly seen the oppression of my people in Egypt. I have heard their groans and have come down to rescue them. Now go, for I am sending you back to Egypt.'

35 "So God sent back the same man his people had previously rejected when they demanded, 'Who made you a ruler and judge over us?' Through the angel who appeared to him in the burning bush, God sent Moses to be their ruler and savior. 36 And by means of many wonders and miraculous signs, he led them out of Egypt, through the Red Sea, and through the wilderness for forty years.

37 "Moses himself told the people of Israel, 'God will raise up for you a Prophet like me from among your own people.' 38 Moses was with our ancestors, the assembly of God's people in the wilderness, when the angel spoke to him at Mount Sinai. And there Moses received life-giving words to pass on to us.

39 "But our ancestors refused to listen to Moses. They rejected him and wanted to return to Egypt. 40 They told Aaron, 'Make us some gods who can lead us, for we don't know what has become of this Moses, who brought us out of Egypt.' 41 So they made an idol shaped like a calf, and they sacrificed to it and celebrated over this thing they had made. 42 Then God turned away from them and abandoned them to serve the stars of heaven as their gods! In the book of the prophets it is written,

Jesus is at God's side to receive the honor due him as hero-savior of the world. He sent his Holy Spirit to live in us. Bring it on.

© ORCEA DAVID/PHOTOS.COM

'Was it to me you were bringing
sacrifices and offerings
during those forty years in the
wilderness, Israel?
⁴³ No, you carried your pagan gods—
the shrine of Molech,
the star of your god Rephan,
and the images you made to
worship them.
So I will send you into exile
as far away as Babylon.'

⁴⁴"Our ancestors carried the Tabernacle with them through the wilderness. It was constructed according to the plan God had shown to Moses. ⁴⁵Years later, when Joshua led our ancestors in battle against the nations that God drove out of this land, the Tabernacle was taken with them into their new territory. And it stayed there until the time of King David.

⁴⁶"David found favor with God and asked for the privilege of building a permanent Temple for the God of Jacob. ⁴⁷But it was Solomon who actually built it. ⁴⁸However, the Most High doesn't live in temples made by human hands. As the prophet says,

⁴⁹ 'Heaven is my throne,
and the earth is my footstool.
Could you build me a temple as
good as that?'
asks the LORD.
'Could you build me such a resting
place?
⁵⁰   Didn't my hands make both
heaven and earth?'

⁵¹"You stubborn people! You are heathen at heart and deaf to the truth. Must you forever resist the Holy Spirit? That's what your ancestors did, and so do you! ⁵²Name one prophet your ancestors didn't persecute! They even killed the ones who predicted the coming of the Righteous One—the Messiah whom you betrayed and murdered. ⁵³You deliberately disobeyed God's law, even though you received it from the hands of angels."

⁵⁴The Jewish leaders were infuriated by Stephen's accusation, and they shook their fists at him in rage. ⁵⁵But Stephen, full of the Holy Spirit, gazed steadily into heaven and saw the glory of God, and he saw Jesus standing in the place of honor at God's right hand. ⁵⁶And he told them, "Look, I see the heavens opened and the Son of Man standing in the place of honor at God's right hand!"

⁵⁷Then they put their hands over their ears and began shouting. They rushed at him ⁵⁸and dragged him out of the city and began to stone him. His accusers took off their coats and laid them at the feet of a young man named Saul.

⁵⁹As they stoned him, Stephen prayed, "Lord Jesus, receive my spirit." ⁶⁰He fell to his knees, shouting, "Lord, don't charge them with this sin!" And with that, he died.
⁸:¹Saul was one of the witnesses, and he agreed completely with the killing of Stephen.

Persecution Scatters the Believers

A great wave of persecution began that day, sweeping over the church in Jerusalem; and all the believers except the apostles were scattered through the regions of Judea and Samaria. ²(Some devout men came and buried Stephen with great mourning.) ³But Saul was going everywhere to destroy the church. He went from house to house, dragging out both men and women to throw them into prison.

The Message of Jesus Spreads

⁴But the believers who were scattered preached the Good News about Jesus wherever they went. ⁵Philip, for example, went to the city of Samaria and told the people there about the Messiah. ⁶Crowds listened intently to Philip because they were eager to hear his message and see the miraculous signs he did. ⁷Many evil spirits were cast out, screaming as they left their victims. And many who had been paralyzed or lame were healed. ⁸So there was great joy in that city.

⁹A man named Simon had been a sorcerer there for many years, amazing the people of Samaria and claiming to be someone great. ¹⁰Everyone, from the least to the greatest, often spoke of him as "the Great One—the Power of God." ¹¹They listened closely to him because for a long time he had astounded them with his magic.

¹²But now the people believed Philip's message of Good News concerning the Kingdom of God and the name of Jesus Christ. As a result, many men and women were baptized. ¹³Then Simon himself believed and was baptized. He began following Philip wherever he went, and he was amazed by the signs and great miracles Philip performed.

¹⁴When the apostles in Jerusalem heard that the people of Samaria had accepted God's message, they sent Peter and John there. ¹⁵As soon as they arrived, they prayed for these new believers to receive the Holy Spirit. ¹⁶The Holy Spirit had not yet come upon any of them, for they had only been baptized in the name of the Lord Jesus. ¹⁷Then Peter and John laid their hands upon these believers, and they received the Holy Spirit.

¹⁸When Simon saw that the Spirit was given when the apostles laid their hands on people, he offered them money to buy this power. ¹⁹"Let me have this power, too," he exclaimed, "so that when I lay my hands on people, they will receive the Holy Spirit!"

²⁰But Peter replied, "May your money be destroyed with you for thinking God's gift can be bought! ²¹You can have no part in this, for your heart is not right with God. ²²Repent of your wickedness and pray to the Lord. Perhaps he will forgive your evil thoughts, ²³for I can see that you are full of bitter jealousy and are held captive by sin."

²⁴"Pray to the Lord for me," Simon exclaimed, "that these terrible things you've said won't happen to me!"

²⁵After testifying and preaching the word of the Lord in Samaria, Peter and John returned to Jerusalem. And they stopped in many Samaritan villages along the way to preach the Good News.

Philip and the Ethiopian Politician

²⁶As for Philip, an angel of the Lord said to him, "Go south down the desert road that runs from Jerusalem to Gaza." ²⁷So he started out, and he met the treasurer of Ethiopia, a eunuch of great authority under the Kandake, the queen of Ethiopia. The eunuch had gone to

Jerusalem to worship, 28 and he was now returning. Seated in his carriage, he was reading aloud from the book of the prophet Isaiah.

29 The Holy Spirit said to Philip, "Go over and walk along beside the carriage."

30 Philip ran over and heard the man reading from the prophet Isaiah. Philip asked, "Do you understand what you are reading?"

31 The man replied, "How can I, unless someone instructs me?" And he urged Philip to come up into the carriage and sit with him.

32 The passage of Scripture he had been reading was this:

"He was led like a sheep to the slaughter.
And as a lamb is silent before the shearers,
he did not open his mouth.
33 He was humiliated and received no justice.
Who can speak of his descendants?
For his life was taken from the earth."

34 The eunuch asked Philip, "Tell me, was the prophet talking about himself or someone else?" 35 So beginning with this same Scripture, Philip told him the Good News about Jesus.

36 As they rode along, they came to some water, and the eunuch said, "Look! There's some water! Why can't I be baptized?" 38 He ordered the carriage to stop, and they went down into the water, and Philip baptized him.

39 When they came up out of the water, the Spirit of the Lord snatched Philip away. The eunuch never saw him again but went on his way rejoicing. 40 Meanwhile, Philip found himself farther north at the town of Azotus. He preached the Good News there and in every town along the way until he came to Caesarea.

Following Jesus is an on-your-toes daily adventure. Once we start to respond to his direction in our lives, we should be ready for anything. Are you up for this?

Saul Is Confronted by Jesus

9:1 Meanwhile, Saul was uttering threats with every breath and was eager to kill the Lord's followers. So he went to the high priest. 2 He requested letters addressed to the synagogues in Damascus, asking for their cooperation in the arrest of any followers of the Way he found there. He wanted to bring them—both men and women—back to Jerusalem in chains.

3 As he was approaching Damascus on this mission, a light from heaven suddenly shone down around him. 4 He fell to the ground and heard a voice saying to him, "Saul! Saul! Why are you persecuting me?"

5 "Who are you, lord?" Saul asked.

And the voice replied, "I am Jesus, the one you are persecuting! 6 Now get up and go into the city, and you will be told what you must do."

7 The men with Saul stood speechless, for they heard the sound of someone's voice but saw no one! 8 Saul picked himself up off the ground, but when he opened his eyes he was blind. So his companions led him by the hand to Damascus. 9 He remained there blind for three days and did not eat or drink.

10 Now there was a believer in Damascus named Ananias. The Lord spoke to him in a vision, calling, "Ananias!"

"Yes, Lord!" he replied.

11 The Lord said, "Go over to Straight Street, to the house of Judas. When you get there, ask for a man from Tarsus named Saul. He is praying to me right now. 12 I have shown him a vision of a man named Ananias coming in and laying hands on him so he can see again."

13 "But Lord," exclaimed Ananias, "I've heard many people talk about the terrible things this man has done to the believers in Jerusalem! 14 And he is authorized by the leading priests to arrest everyone who calls upon your name."

15 But the Lord said, "Go, for Saul is my chosen instrument to take my message to the Gentiles and to kings, as well as to the people of Israel. 16 And I will show him how much he must suffer for my name's sake."

17 So Ananias went and found Saul. He laid his hands on him and said, "Brother Saul, the Lord Jesus, who appeared to you on the road, has sent me so that you might regain your sight and be filled with the Holy Spirit." 18 Instantly something like scales fell from Saul's eyes, and he regained his sight.

Then he got up and was baptized. 19 Afterward he ate some food and regained his strength.

Saul in Damascus and Jerusalem

Saul stayed with the believers in Damascus for a few days. 20 And immediately he began preaching about Jesus in the synagogues, saying, "He is indeed the Son of God!"

21 All who heard him were amazed. "Isn't this the same man who caused such devastation among Jesus' followers in Jerusalem?" they asked. "And didn't he come here to arrest them and take them in chains to the leading priests?"

22 Saul's preaching became more and more powerful, and the Jews in Damascus couldn't refute his proofs that Jesus was indeed the Messiah. 23 After a while some of the Jews plotted together to kill him. 24 They were watching for him day and night at the city gate so they could murder him, but Saul was told about their plot. 25 So during the night, some of the other believers lowered him in a large basket through an opening in the city wall.

26 When Saul arrived in Jerusalem, he tried to meet with the believers, but they were all afraid of him. They did not believe he had truly become a believer! 27 Then Barnabas brought him to the apostles and told them how Saul had seen the Lord on the way to Damascus and how the Lord had spoken to Saul. He also told them that Saul had preached boldly in the name of Jesus in Damascus.

28 So Saul stayed with the apostles and went all around Jerusalem with them, preaching boldly in the name

Jesus is able to fight his own battles. He specializes in reversing the course of enemies so that they become dedicated followers.

of the Lord. ²⁹He debated with some Greek-speaking Jews, but they tried to murder him. ³⁰When the believers heard about this, they took him down to Caesarea and sent him away to Tarsus, his hometown.

³¹The church then had peace throughout Judea, Galilee, and Samaria, and it became stronger as the believers lived in the fear of the Lord. And with the encouragement of the Holy Spirit, it also grew in numbers.

Peter Heals Aeneas and Raises Dorcas

³²Meanwhile, Peter traveled from place to place, and he came down to visit the believers in the town of Lydda. ³³There believers had heard that Peter was nearby at Lydda, so they sent two men to beg him, "Please come as soon as possible!"

³⁹So Peter returned with them; and as soon as he arrived, they took him to the upstairs room. The room was filled with widows who were weeping and showing him the coats and other clothes Dorcas had made for them. ⁴⁰But Peter asked them all to leave the room; then he knelt and prayed. Turning to the body he said, "Get up, Tabitha." And she opened her eyes! When she saw Peter, she sat up! ⁴¹He gave her his hand and helped her up. Then he called in the widows and all the believers, and he presented her to them alive.

> As far as miracles go, it's pretty tough to do better than raising someone from the dead. Jesus said his followers would do greater works than he did; what might he do through you?

he met a man named Aeneas, who had been paralyzed and bedridden for eight years. ³⁴Peter said to him, "Aeneas, Jesus Christ heals you! Get up, and roll up your sleeping mat!" And he was healed instantly. ³⁵Then the whole population of Lydda and Sharon saw Aeneas walking around, and they turned to the Lord.

³⁶There was a believer in Joppa named Tabitha (which in Greek is Dorcas). She was always doing kind things for others and helping the poor. ³⁷About this time she became ill and died. Her body was washed for burial and laid in an upstairs room. ³⁸But the

⁴²The news spread through the whole town, and many believed in the Lord. ⁴³And Peter stayed a long time in Joppa, living with Simon, a tanner of hides.

Cornelius Calls for Peter

¹⁰:¹In Caesarea there lived a Roman army named Cornelius, who was a captain of the Italian Regiment. ²He was a devout, God-fearing man, as was everyone in his household. He gave generously to the poor and prayed regularly to God. ³One afternoon about three o'clock, he had a vision in which he saw an angel of God coming toward him. "Cornelius!" the angel said.

⁴Cornelius stared at him in terror. "What is it, sir?" he asked the angel.

And the angel replied, "Your prayers and gifts to the poor have been received by God as an offering! ⁵Now send some men to Joppa, and summon a man named Simon Peter. ⁶He is staying with Simon, a tanner who lives near the seashore."

⁷As soon as the angel was gone, Cornelius called two of his household servants and a devout soldier, one of his personal attendants. ⁸He told them what had happened and sent them off to Joppa.

Peter Visits Cornelius

⁹The next day as Cornelius's messengers were nearing the town, Peter went up on the flat roof to pray. It was about noon, ¹⁰and he was hungry. But while a meal was being prepared, he fell into a trance. ¹¹He saw the sky open, and something like a large sheet was let down by its four corners. ¹²In the sheet were all sorts of animals, reptiles, and birds. ¹³Then a voice said to him, "Get up, Peter; kill and eat them."

¹⁴"No, Lord," Peter declared. "I have never eaten anything that our Jewish laws have declared impure and unclean."

¹⁵But the voice spoke again: "Do not call something unclean if God has made it clean." ¹⁶The same vision was repeated three times. Then the sheet was suddenly pulled up to heaven.

¹⁷Peter was very perplexed. What could the vision mean? Just then the men sent by Cornelius found Simon's house. Standing outside the gate, ¹⁸they asked if a man named Simon Peter was staying there.

¹⁹Meanwhile, as Peter was puzzling over the vision, the Holy Spirit said to him, "Three men have come looking for you. ²⁰Get up, go downstairs, and go with them without hesitation. Don't worry, for I have sent them."

²¹So Peter went down and said, "I'm the man you are looking for. Why have you come?"

²²They said, "We were sent by Cornelius, a Roman officer. He is a devout and God-fearing man, well respected by all the Jews. A holy angel instructed him to summon you to his house so that he can hear your message." ²³So Peter invited the men to stay for the night. The next day he went with them, accompanied by some of the brothers from Joppa.

²⁴They arrived in Caesarea the following day. Cornelius was waiting for them and had called together his relatives and close friends. ²⁵As Peter entered his home, Cornelius fell at his feet and worshiped him. ²⁶But Peter pulled him up and said, "Stand up! I'm a human being just like you!" ²⁷So they talked together and went inside, where many others were assembled.

²⁸Peter told them, "You know it is against our laws for a Jewish man to enter a Gentile home like this or to associate with you. But God has shown me that I should no longer think of anyone as impure or unclean. ²⁹So I came without objection as soon as I was sent for. Now tell me why you sent for me."

³⁰Cornelius replied, "Four days ago I was praying in my house about this same time, three o'clock in the afternoon. Suddenly, a man in dazzling clothes was standing in front of me. ³¹He told me, 'Cornelius, your prayer

has been heard, and your gifts to the poor have been noticed by God! ³²Now send messengers to Joppa, and summon a man named Simon Peter. He is staying in the home of Simon, a tanner who lives near the seashore.' ³³So I sent for you at once, and it was good of you to come. Now we are all here, waiting before God to hear the message the Lord has given you."

The Good News Shared with Outsiders

³⁴Then Peter replied, "I see very clearly that God shows no favoritism. ³⁵In every nation he accepts those who fear him and do what is right. ³⁶This is the message of Good News for the people of Israel—that there is peace with God through Jesus Christ, who is Lord of all. ³⁷You know what happened throughout Judea, beginning in Galilee, after John began preaching his message of baptism. ³⁸And you know that God anointed Jesus of Nazareth with the Holy Spirit and with power. Then Jesus went around doing good and healing all who were oppressed by the devil, for God was with him.

³⁹"And we apostles are witnesses of all he did throughout Judea and in Jerusalem. They put him to death by hanging him on a cross, ⁴⁰but God raised him to life on the third day. Then God allowed him to appear, ⁴¹not to the general public, but to us whom God had chosen in advance to be his witnesses. We were those who ate and drank with him after he rose from the dead. ⁴²And he ordered us to preach everywhere and to testify that Jesus is the one appointed by God to be the judge of all—the living and the dead.

⁴³He is the one all the prophets testified about, saying that everyone who believes in him will have their sins forgiven through his name."

Outsiders Receive the Holy Spirit

⁴⁴Even as Peter was saying these things, the Holy Spirit fell upon all who were listening to the message. ⁴⁵The Jewish believers who came with Peter were amazed that the gift of the Holy Spirit had been poured out on the Gentiles, too. ⁴⁶For they heard them speaking in other tongues and praising God.

Then Peter asked, ⁴⁷"Can anyone object to their being baptized, now that they have received the Holy Spirit just as we did?" ⁴⁸So he gave orders for them to be baptized in the name of Jesus Christ. Afterward Cornelius asked him to stay with them for several days.

Peter Explains His Actions

11:1 Soon the news reached the apostles and other believers in Judea that the Gentiles had received the word of God. ²But when Peter arrived back in Jerusalem, the Jewish believers criticized him. ³"You entered the home of Gentiles and even ate with them!" they said.

⁴Then Peter told them exactly what had happened. ⁵"I was in the town of Joppa," he said, "and while I was praying, I went into a trance and saw a vision. Something like a large sheet was let down by its four corners from the sky. And it came right down to me. ⁶When I looked inside the sheet, I saw all sorts of tame and wild animals, reptiles, and birds. ⁷And I heard a voice say, 'Get up, Peter; kill and eat them.'

⁸"'No, Lord,' I replied. 'I have never eaten anything that our Jewish laws have declared impure or unclean.'

⁹"But the voice from heaven spoke again: 'Do not call something unclean if God has made it clean.' ¹⁰This happened three times before the sheet and all it contained was pulled back up to heaven.

¹¹"Just then three men who had been sent from Caesarea arrived at the house where we were staying. ¹²The Holy Spirit told me to go with them and not to worry that they were Gentiles. These six brothers here accompanied me, and we soon entered the home of the man who had sent for us. ¹³He told us how an angel had appeared to him in his home and had told him, 'Send messengers to Joppa, and summon a man named Simon Peter. ¹⁴He will tell you how you and everyone in your household can be saved!'

of repenting of their sins and receiving eternal life."

The Church in Antioch of Syria

¹⁹Meanwhile, the believers who had been scattered during the persecution after Stephen's death traveled as far as Phoenicia, Cyprus, and Antioch of Syria. They preached the word of God, but only to Jews. ²⁰However, some of the believers who went to Antioch from Cyprus and Cyrene began preaching to the Gentiles about the Lord Jesus. ²¹The power of the Lord was with them, and a large number of these Gentiles believed and turned to the Lord.

²²When the church at Jerusalem heard what had happened, they sent Barnabas to Antioch. ²³When he arrived and saw this evidence of God's

> Jesus will mess up our old way of thinking in order to help us see things from his point of view. What are some things you've learned in your life that may need to be unlearned?

¹⁵"As I began to speak," Peter continued, "the Holy Spirit fell on them, just as he fell on us at the beginning. ¹⁶Then I thought of the Lord's words when he said, 'John baptized with water, but you will be baptized with the Holy Spirit.' ¹⁷And since God gave these Gentiles the same gift he gave us when we believed in the Lord Jesus Christ, who was I to stand in God's way?"

¹⁸When the others heard this, they stopped objecting and began praising God. They said, "We can see that God has also given the Gentiles the privilege

blessing, he was filled with joy, and he encouraged the believers to stay true to the Lord. ²⁴Barnabas was a good man, full of the Holy Spirit and strong in faith. And many people were brought to the Lord.

²⁵Then Barnabas went on to Tarsus to look for Saul. ²⁶When he found him, he brought him back to Antioch. Both of them stayed there with the church for a full year, teaching large crowds of people. (It was at Antioch that the believers were first called Christians.)

LETTERS FROM JESUS' EARLIEST FOLLOWERS

Jesus gave his followers a mission: to spread his message all over the world. As the earliest followers of Jesus traveled with his message they grew in number. Churches—groups of followers that frequently came together to worship God and help each other live out their new life with Jesus—popped up everywhere. Leaders soon discovered the value of writing letters to teach and encourage these new Christians. Twenty-one of these letters remain a part of the Bible today. Some are short; others are pretty long. All of them provide instructions to guide Christians into a deeper understanding of Jesus and how to follow him.

Nobody wrote more of these letters than the apostle Paul. You might remember him as Saul, the guy we read about in Acts 9:1-31 (pages 83-86). He became a great ambassador for Jesus all over the known world, and his letters to Christ's followers back in the day make up almost half of the books in the New Testament portion of the Bible. Here's just a sample of what's in those letters:

But God showed his great love for us by sending Christ to die for us while we were still sinners. **Romans 5:8**

And I am convinced that nothing can ever separate us from God's love. Neither death nor life, neither angels nor demons, neither our fears for today nor our worries about tomorrow—not even the powers of hell can separate us from God's love. No power in the sky above or in the earth below—indeed, nothing in all creation will ever be able to separate us from the love of God that is revealed in Christ Jesus our Lord. **Romans 8:38-39**

Don't copy the behavior and customs of this world, but let God transform you into a new person by changing the way you think. Then you will learn to know God's will for you, which is good and pleasing and perfect. **Romans 12:2**

Love is patient and kind. Love is not jealous or boastful or proud or rude. It does not demand its own way. It is not irritable, and it keeps no record of being wronged. It does not rejoice about injustice but rejoices whenever the truth wins out. Love never gives up, never loses faith, is always hopeful, and endures through every circumstance. **1 Corinthians 13:4-7**

But the Holy Spirit produces this kind of fruit in our lives: love, joy, peace, patience, kindness, goodness, faithfulness, gentleness, and self-control. There is no law against these things! **Galatians 5:22-23**

Then Christ will make his home in your hearts as you trust in him. Your roots will grow down into God's love and keep you strong. And may you have the power to understand, as all God's people should, how wide, how long, how high, and how deep his love is. May you experience the love of Christ, though it is too great to understand fully. Then you will be made complete with all the fullness of life and power that comes from God. **Ephesians 3:17-19**

Christ is the visible image of the invisible God. He existed before anything was created and is supreme over all creation, for through him God created everything in the heavenly realms and on earth. He made the things we can see and the things we can't see—such as thrones, kingdoms, rulers, and authorities in the unseen world. Everything was created through him and for him. He existed before anything else, and he holds all creation together. Christ is also the head of the church, which is his body. He is the beginning, supreme over all who rise from the dead. So he is first in everything. For God in all his fullness was pleased to live in Christ, and through him God reconciled everything to himself. He made peace with everything in heaven and on earth by means of Christ's blood on the cross. **Colossians 1:15-20**

Curious about the sort of changes that happen for those who trust in Jesus? Read the two letters that start on the next page. Neither of them were written by Paul, but both of them will give you a clear picture of what it looks like to follow Jesus.

THE BOOK OF JAMES

This letter, written by the early church leader James, offers lots of practical advice for making sure our faith actually shows up in what we say and do. What good is faith in Jesus if it makes no difference in the way you live? As James says, it would be useless.

James, Brother of Jesus, Teaches about True Faith

1:1 This letter is from James, a slave of God and of the Lord Jesus Christ.

I am writing to the "twelve tribes"—Jewish believers scattered abroad.

Greetings!

Faith and Endurance

2 Dear brothers and sisters, when troubles of any kind come your way, consider it an opportunity for great joy. 3 For you know that when your faith is tested, your endurance has a chance to grow. 4 So let it grow, for when your endurance is fully developed, you will be perfect and complete, needing nothing.

5 If you need wisdom, ask our generous God, and he will give it to you. He will not rebuke you for asking. 6 But when you ask him, be sure that your faith is in God alone. Do not waver, for a person with divided loyalty is as unsettled as a wave of the sea that is blown and tossed by the wind. 7 Such people should not expect to receive anything from the Lord. 8 Their loyalty is divided between God and the world, and they are unstable in everything they do.

9 Believers who are poor have something to boast about, for God has honored them. 10 And those who are rich should boast that God has humbled them. They will fade away like a little flower in the field. 11 The hot sun rises and the grass withers; the little flower droops and falls, and its beauty fades away. In the same way, the rich will fade away with all of their achievements.

12 God blesses those who patiently endure testing and temptation. Afterward they will receive the crown of life that God has promised to those who love him. 13 And remember, when you are being tempted, do not say, "God is tempting me." God is never tempted to do wrong, and he never tempts anyone else. 14 Temptation comes from our own desires, which entice us and drag us away. 15 These desires give birth to sinful actions. And when sin is allowed to grow, it gives birth to death.

16 So don't be misled, my dear brothers and sisters. 17 Whatever is good and perfect is a gift coming down to us from God our Father, who created all the lights in the heavens. He never changes or casts a shifting shadow. 18 He chose to give birth to us by giving us his true word. And we, out of all creation, became his prized possession.

Listening and Doing

[19]Understand this, my dear brothers and sisters: You must all be quick to listen, slow to speak, and slow to get angry. [20]Human anger does not produce the righteousness God desires. [21]So get rid of all the filth and evil in your lives, and humbly accept the word God has planted in your hearts, for it has the power to save your souls.

[22]But don't just listen to God's word. You must do what it says. Otherwise, you are only fooling yourselves. [23]For if you listen to the word and don't obey, it is like glancing at your face in a mirror. [24]You see yourself, walk away, and forget what you look like. [25]But if you look carefully into the perfect law that sets you free, and if you do what it says and don't forget what you heard, then God will bless you for doing it.

[26]If you claim to be religious but don't control your tongue, you are fooling yourself, and your religion is worthless. [27]Pure and genuine religion in the sight of God the Father means caring for orphans and widows in their distress and refusing to let the world corrupt you.

A Warning against Prejudice

[2:1]My dear brothers and sisters, how can you claim to have faith in our glorious Lord Jesus Christ if you favor some people over others?

[2]For example, suppose someone comes into your meeting dressed in fancy clothes and expensive jewelry, and another comes in who is poor and dressed in dirty clothes. [3]If you give special attention and a good seat to the rich person, but you say to the poor one, "You can stand over there, or else sit on the floor"—well, [4]doesn't this discrimination show that your judgments are guided by evil motives?

[5]Listen to me, dear brothers and sisters. Hasn't God chosen the poor in this world to be rich in faith? Aren't they the ones who will inherit the Kingdom he promised to those who love him? [6]But you dishonor the poor! Isn't it the rich who oppress you and drag you into court? [7]Aren't they the ones who slander Jesus Christ, whose noble name you bear?

[8]Yes indeed, it is good when you obey the royal law as found in the Scriptures: "Love your neighbor as yourself." [9]But if you favor some people over others, you are committing a sin. You are guilty of breaking the law.

[10]For the person who keeps all of the laws except one is as guilty as a person who has broken all of God's laws. [11]For the same God who said, "You must not commit adultery," also said, "You must not murder." So if you murder someone but do not commit adultery, you have still broken the law.

[12]So whatever you say or whatever you do, remember that you will be judged by the law that sets you free. [13]There will be no mercy for those who have not shown mercy to others. But if you have been merciful, God will be merciful when he judges you.

Faith without Good Deeds Is Dead

[14]What good is it, dear brothers and sisters, if you say you have faith but don't show it by your actions? Can that kind of faith save anyone? [15]Suppose you see a brother or sister who has no food or clothing, [16]and you say, "Goodbye and have a good day; stay warm

and eat well"—but then you don't give that person any food or clothing. What good does that do?

17 So you see, faith by itself isn't enough. Unless it produces good deeds, it is dead and useless.

18 Now someone may argue, "Some people have faith; others have good deeds." But I say, "How can you show me your faith if you don't have good deeds? I will show you my faith by my good deeds."

19 You say you have faith, for you believe that there is one God. Good for you! Even the demons believe this, and they tremble in terror. 20 How foolish! Can't you see that faith without good deeds is useless?

21 Don't you remember that our ancestor Abraham was shown to be right with God by his actions when he offered his son Isaac on the altar? 22 You see, his faith and his actions worked together. His actions made his faith complete. 23 And so it happened just as the Scriptures say: "Abraham believed God, and God counted him as righteous because of his faith." He was even called the friend of God. 24 So you see, we are shown to be right with God by what we do, not by faith alone.

25 Rahab the prostitute is another example. She was shown to be right with God by her actions when she hid those messengers and sent them safely away by a different road. 26 Just as the body is dead without breath, so also faith is dead without good works.

Controlling the Tongue

3:1 Dear brothers and sisters, not many of you should become teachers in the church, for we who teach will be judged more strictly. 2 Indeed, we all make many mistakes. For if we could control our tongues, we would be perfect and could also control ourselves in every other way.

3 We can make a large horse go wherever we want by means of a small bit in its mouth. 4 And a small rudder makes a huge ship turn wherever the pilot chooses to go, even though the winds are strong. 5 In the same way, the tongue is a small thing that makes grand speeches.

But a tiny spark can set a great forest on fire. 6 And among all the parts of the body, the tongue is a flame of fire. It is a whole world of wickedness, corrupting your entire body. It can set your whole life on fire, for it is set on fire by hell itself.

7 People can tame all kinds of animals, birds, reptiles, and fish, 8 but no one can tame the tongue. It is restless and evil, full of deadly poison. 9 Sometimes it praises our Lord and Father, and sometimes it curses those who have been made in the image of God. 10 And so blessing and cursing come pouring out of the same mouth. Surely, my brothers and sisters, this is not right! 11 Does a spring of water bubble out with both fresh water and bitter water? 12 Does a fig tree produce olives, or a grapevine produce figs? No, and you can't draw fresh water from a salty spring.

True Wisdom Comes from God

13 If you are wise and understand God's ways, prove it by living an honorable life, doing good works with the humility that comes from wisdom. 14 But if you are bitterly jealous and there is

> Jesus is the kind of speech teacher we all need. He forms our heart into something good so that what comes out of our mouths is worthwhile.

selfish ambition in your heart, don't cover up the truth with boasting and lying. [15]For jealousy and selfishness are not God's kind of wisdom. Such things are earthly, unspiritual, and demonic. [16]For wherever there is jealousy and selfish ambition, there you will find disorder and evil of every kind.

[17]But the wisdom from above is first of all pure. It is also peace loving, gentle at all times, and willing to yield to others. It is full of mercy and the fruit of good deeds. It shows no favoritism and is always sincere. [18]And those who are peacemakers will plant seeds of peace and reap a harvest of righteousness.

Drawing Close to God

[4:1]What is causing the quarrels and fights among you? Don't they come from the evil desires at war within you? [2]You want what you don't have, so you scheme and kill to get it. You are jealous of what others have, but you can't get it, so you fight and wage war to take it away from them. Yet you don't have what you want because you don't ask

God for it. [3]And even when you ask, you don't get it because your motives are all wrong—you want only what will give you pleasure.

[4]You adulterers! Don't you realize that friendship with the world makes you an enemy of God? I say it again: If you want to be a friend of the world, you make yourself an enemy of God. [5]Do you think the Scriptures have no meaning? They say that God is passionate that the spirit he has placed within us should be faithful to him. [6]And he gives grace generously. As the Scriptures say,

"God opposes the proud
  but gives grace to the humble."

[7]So humble yourselves before God. Resist the devil, and he will flee from you. [8]Come close to God, and God will come close to you. Wash your hands, you sinners; purify your hearts, for your loyalty is divided between God and the world. [9]Let there be tears for what you have done. Let there be sorrow and deep grief. Let there be sadness instead of laughter, and gloom instead of joy. [10]Humble yourselves before the Lord, and he will lift you up in honor.

Warning against Judging Others

[11]Don't speak evil against each other, dear brothers and sisters. If you criticize and judge each other, then you are criticizing and judging God's law. But your job is to obey the law, not to judge whether it applies to you. [12]God alone, who gave the law, is the Judge. He alone has the power to save or to destroy. So what right do you have to judge your neighbor?

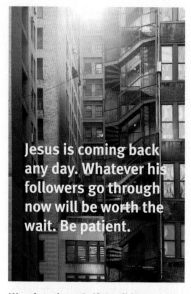

Jesus is coming back any day. Whatever his followers go through now will be worth the wait. Be patient.

Warning about Self-Confidence

¹³Look here, you who say, "Today or tomorrow we are going to a certain town and will stay there a year. We will do business there and make a profit." ¹⁴How do you know what your life will be like tomorrow? Your life is like the morning fog—it's here a little while, then it's gone. ¹⁵What you ought to say is, "If the Lord wants us to, we will live and do this or that." ¹⁶Otherwise you are boasting about your own pretentious plans, and all such boasting is evil.

¹⁷Remember, it is sin to know what you ought to do and then not do it.

Warning to the Rich

⁵:¹Look here, you rich people: Weep and groan with anguish because of all the terrible troubles ahead of you. ²Your wealth is rotting away, and your fine clothes are moth-eaten rags. ³Your gold and silver are corroded. The very wealth you were counting on will eat away your flesh like fire. This corroded treasure you have hoarded will testify against you on the day of judgment. ⁴For listen! Hear the cries of the field workers whom you have cheated of their pay. The cries of those who harvest your fields have reached the ears of the LORD of Heaven's Armies.

⁵You have spent your years on earth in luxury, satisfying your every desire. You have fattened yourselves for the day of slaughter. ⁶You have condemned and killed innocent people, who do not resist you.

Patience and Endurance

⁷Dear brothers and sisters, be patient as you wait for the Lord's return. Consider the farmers who patiently wait for the rains in the fall and in the spring. They eagerly look for the valuable harvest to ripen. ⁸You, too, must be patient. Take courage, for the coming of the Lord is near.

⁹Don't grumble about each other, brothers and sisters, or you will be judged. For look—the Judge is standing at the door!

¹⁰For examples of patience in suffering, dear brothers and sisters, look at the prophets who spoke in the name of the Lord. ¹¹We give great honor to those who endure under suffering. For instance, you know about Job, a man of great endurance. You can see how the Lord was kind to him at the end, for the Lord is full of tenderness and mercy.

¹²But most of all, my brothers and sisters, never take an oath, by heaven or earth or anything else. Just say a

simple yes or no, so that you will not sin and be condemned.

The Power of Prayer

[13] Are any of you suffering hardships? You should pray. Are any of you happy? You should sing praises. [14] Are any of you sick? You should call for the elders of the church to come and pray over you, anointing you with oil in the name of the Lord. [15] Such a prayer offered in faith will heal the sick, and the Lord will make you well. And if you have committed any sins, you will be forgiven.

[16] Confess your sins to each other and pray for each other so that you may be healed. The earnest prayer of a righteous person has great power and produces wonderful results. [17] Elijah was as human as we are, and yet when he prayed earnestly that no rain would fall, none fell for three and a half years! [18] Then, when he prayed again, the sky sent down rain and the earth began to yield its crops.

Restore Wandering Believers

[19] My dear brothers and sisters, if someone among you wanders away from the truth and is brought back, [20] you can be sure that whoever brings the sinner back from wandering will save that person from death and bring about the forgiveness of many sins.

THE BOOK OF FIRST JOHN

This is the first of three letters written by our Gospel writer, John. Simple and focused, John shows us how the love and truth Jesus gives us combine to create in us a life that's full of joy and points others to Jesus.

John Writes about Living as a Follower of Jesus

[1:1] We proclaim to you the one who existed from the beginning, whom we have heard and seen. We saw him with our own eyes and touched him with our own hands. He is the Word of life. [2] This one who is life itself was revealed to us, and we have seen him. And now we testify and proclaim to you that he is the one who is eternal life. He was with the Father, and then he was revealed to us. [3] We proclaim to you what we ourselves have actually seen and heard so that you may have fellowship with us. And our fellowship is with the Father and with his Son, Jesus Christ. [4] We are writing these things so that you may fully share our joy.

Living in the Light

[5] This is the message we heard from Jesus and now declare to you: God is light, and there is no darkness in him at all. [6] So we are lying if we say we have fellowship with God but go on living in spiritual darkness; we are

not practicing the truth. [7]But if we are living in the light, as God is in the light, then we have fellowship with each other, and the blood of Jesus, his Son, cleanses us from all sin.

[8]If we claim we have no sin, we are only fooling ourselves and not living in the truth. [9]But if we confess our sins to him, he is faithful and just to forgive us our sins and to cleanse us from all wickedness. [10]If we claim we have not sinned, we are calling God a liar and showing that his word has no place in our hearts.

[2:1]My dear children, I am writing this to you so that you will not sin. But if anyone does sin, we have an advocate who pleads our case before the Father. He is Jesus Christ, the one who is truly righteous. [2]He himself is the sacrifice that atones for our sins—and not only our sins but the sins of all the world.

[3]And we can be sure that we know him if we obey his commandments. [4]If someone claims, "I know God," but doesn't obey God's commandments, that person is a liar and is not living in the truth. [5]But those who obey God's word truly show how completely they love him. That is how we know we are living in him. [6]Those who say they live in God should live their lives as Jesus did.

A New Commandment

[7]Dear friends, I am not writing a new commandment for you; rather it is an old one you have had from the very beginning. This old commandment—to love one another—is the same message you heard before. [8]Yet it is also new. Jesus lived the truth of this commandment, and you also are living it. For the darkness is disappearing, and the true light is already shining.

[9]If anyone claims, "I am living in the light," but hates a fellow believer, that person is still living in darkness. [10]Anyone who loves a fellow believer is living in the light and does not cause others to stumble. [11]But anyone who hates a fellow believer is still living and walking in darkness. Such a person does not know the way to go, having been blinded by the darkness.

[12] I am writing to you who are God's children
   because your sins have been forgiven through Jesus.
[13] I am writing to you who are mature in the faith
   because you know Christ, who existed from the beginning.
   I am writing to you who are young in the faith
   because you have won your battle with the evil one.
[14] I have written to you who are God's children
   because you know the Father.
   I have written to you who are mature in the faith
   because you know Christ, who existed from the beginning.
   I have written to you who are young in the faith
   because you are strong.
   God's word lives in your hearts,
   and you have won your battle with the evil one.

Do Not Love This World

[15]Do not love this world nor the things it offers you, for when you love the world, you do not have the love of the Father in you. [16]For the world offers only a

craving for physical pleasure, a craving for everything we see, and pride in our achievements and possessions. These are not from the Father, but are from this world. ¹⁷And this world is fading away, along with everything that people crave. But anyone who does what pleases God will live forever.

Warning about Antichrists

¹⁸Dear children, the last hour is here. You have heard that the Antichrist is coming, and already many such antichrists have appeared. From this we know that the last hour has come. ¹⁹These people left our churches, but they never really belonged with us; otherwise they would have stayed with us. When they left, it proved that they did not belong with us.

²⁰But you are not like that, for the Holy One has given you his Spirit, and all of you know the truth. ²¹So I am writing to you not because you don't know the truth but because you know the difference between truth and lies. ²²And who is a liar? Anyone who says that Jesus is not the Christ. Anyone who denies the Father and the Son is an antichrist. ²³Anyone who denies the Son doesn't have the Father, either. But anyone who acknowledges the Son has the Father also.

²⁴So you must remain faithful to what you have been taught from the beginning. If you do, you will remain in fellowship with the Son and with the Father. ²⁵And in this fellowship we enjoy the eternal life he promised us.

²⁶I am writing these things to warn you about those who want to lead you astray. ²⁷But you have received the Holy Spirit, and he lives within you, so you don't need anyone to teach you what is true. For the Spirit teaches you everything you need to know, and what he teaches is true—it is not a lie. So just as he has taught you, remain in fellowship with Christ.

Living as Children of God

²⁸And now, dear children, remain in fellowship with Christ so that when he returns, you will be full of courage and not shrink back from him in shame.

²⁹Since we know that Christ is righteous, we also know that all who do what is right are God's children.

3:1 See how very much our Father loves us, for he calls us his children, and that is what we are! But the people who belong to this world don't recognize that we are God's children because they don't know him. ²Dear friends, we are already God's children, but he has not yet shown us what we will be like when Christ appears. But we do know that we will be like him, for we will see him as he really is. ³And all who have this eager expectation will keep themselves pure, just as he is pure.

⁴Everyone who sins is breaking God's law, for all sin is contrary to the law of God. ⁵And you know that Jesus came to take away our sins, and there is no sin in him. ⁶Anyone who continues to live in him will not sin. But anyone who keeps on sinning does not know him or understand who he is.

⁷Dear children, don't let anyone deceive you about this: When people do what is right, it shows that they are righteous, even as Christ is righteous. ⁸But when people keep on sinning, it shows that they belong to the devil, who has been sinning since the

beginning. But the Son of God came to destroy the works of the devil. ⁹Those who have been born into God's family do not make a practice of sinning, because God's life is in them. So they can't keep on sinning, because they are children of God. ¹⁰So now we can tell who are children of God and who are children of the devil. Anyone who does not live righteously and does not love other believers does not belong to God.

Love One Another

¹¹This is the message you have heard from the beginning: We should love one another. ¹²We must not be like Cain, who belonged to the evil one and killed his brother. And why did he kill him? Because Cain had been doing what was evil, and his brother had been doing what was righteous. ¹³So don't be surprised, dear brothers and sisters, if the world hates you.

¹⁴If we love our brothers and sisters who are believers, it proves that we have passed from death to life. But a person who has no love is still dead. ¹⁵Anyone who hates another brother or sister is really a murderer at heart. And you know that murderers don't have eternal life within them.

¹⁶We know what real love is because Jesus gave up his life for us. So we also ought to give up our lives for our brothers and sisters. ¹⁷If someone has enough money to live well and sees a brother or sister in need but shows no compassion—how can God's love be in that person?

¹⁸Dear children, let's not merely say that we love each other; let us show the truth by our actions. ¹⁹Our actions will show that we belong to the truth, so we will be confident when we stand before God. ²⁰Even if we feel guilty, God is greater than our feelings, and he knows everything.

²¹Dear friends, if we don't feel guilty, we can come to God with bold confidence. ²²And we will receive from him whatever we ask because we obey him and do the things that please him.

²³And this is his commandment: We must believe in the name of his Son, Jesus Christ, and love one another, just as he commanded us. ²⁴Those who obey God's commandments remain in fellowship with him, and he with them. And we know he lives in us because the Spirit he gave us lives in us.

Discerning False Prophets

⁴:¹Dear friends, do not believe everyone who claims to speak by the Spirit. You must test them to see if the spirit they have comes from God. For there are many false prophets in the world. ²This is how we know if they have the Spirit of God: If a person claiming to be a prophet acknowledges that Jesus Christ came in a real body, that person has the Spirit of God. ³But if someone claims to be a prophet and does not acknowledge the truth about Jesus, that person is not from God. Such a person has the spirit of the Antichrist, which you heard is coming into the world and indeed is already here.

⁴But you belong to God, my dear children. You have already won a victory over those people, because the Spirit who lives in you is greater than the spirit who lives in the world. ⁵Those people belong to this world, so they speak from the world's viewpoint, and the world listens to them. ⁶But we

belong to God, and those who know God listen to us. If they do not belong to God, they do not listen to us. That is how we know if someone has the Spirit of truth or the spirit of deception.

Loving One Another

[7]Dear friends, let us continue to love one another, for love comes from God. Anyone who loves is a child of God and knows God. [8]But anyone who does not love does not know God, for God is love.

and his love is brought to full expression in us.

[13]And God has given us his Spirit as proof that we live in him and he in us. [14]Furthermore, we have seen with our own eyes and now testify that the Father sent his Son to be the Savior of the world. [15]All who declare that Jesus is the Son of God have God living in them, and they live in God. [16]We know how much God loves us, and we have put our trust in his love.

God is love, and all who live in love live in God, and God lives in them. [17]And

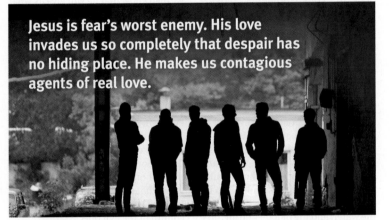

Jesus is fear's worst enemy. His love invades us so completely that despair has no hiding place. He makes us contagious agents of real love.

[9]God showed how much he loved us by sending his one and only Son into the world so that we might have eternal life through him. [10]This is real love—not that we loved God, but that he loved us and sent his Son as a sacrifice to take away our sins.

[11]Dear friends, since God loved us that much, we surely ought to love each other. [12]No one has ever seen God. But if we love each other, God lives in us,

as we live in God, our love grows more perfect. So we will not be afraid on the day of judgment, but we can face him with confidence because we live like Jesus here in this world.

[18]Such love has no fear, because perfect love expels all fear. If we are afraid, it is for fear of punishment, and this shows that we have not fully experienced his perfect love. [19]We love each other because he loved us first.

[20] If someone says, "I love God," but hates a fellow believer, that person is a liar; for if we don't love people we can see, how can we love God, whom we cannot see? [21] And he has given us this command: Those who love God must also love their fellow believers.

Faith in the Son of God

[5:1] Everyone who believes that Jesus is the Christ has become a child of God. And everyone who loves the Father loves his children, too. [2] We know we love God's children if we love God and obey his commandments. [3] Loving God means keeping his commandments, and his commandments are not burdensome. [4] For every child of God defeats this evil world, and we achieve this victory through our faith. [5] And who can win this battle against the world? Only those who believe that Jesus is the Son of God.

[6] And Jesus Christ was revealed as God's Son by his baptism in water and by shedding his blood on the cross—not by water only, but by water and blood. And the Spirit, who is truth, confirms it with his testimony. [7] So we have these three witnesses—[8] the Spirit, the water, and the blood—and all three agree. [9] Since we believe human testimony, surely we can believe the greater testimony that comes from God. And God has testified about his Son. [10] All who believe in the Son of God know in their hearts that this testimony is true. Those who don't believe this are actually calling God a liar because they don't believe what God has testified about his Son.

[11] And this is what God has testified: He has given us eternal life, and this life is in his Son. [12] Whoever has the Son has life; whoever does not have God's Son does not have life.

Conclusion

[13] I have written this to you who believe in the name of the Son of God, so that you may know you have eternal life. [14] And we are confident that he hears us whenever we ask for anything that pleases him. [15] And since we know he hears us when we make our requests, we also know that he will give us what we ask for.

[16] If you see a fellow believer sinning in a way that does not lead to death, you should pray, and God will give that person life. But there is a sin that leads to death, and I am not saying you should pray for those who commit it. [17] All wicked actions are sin, but not every sin leads to death.

[18] We know that God's children do not make a practice of sinning, for God's Son holds them securely, and the evil one cannot touch them. [19] We know that we are children of God and that the world around us is under the control of the evil one.

[20] And we know that the Son of God has come, and he has given us understanding so that we can know the true God. And now we live in fellowship with the true God because we live in fellowship with his Son, Jesus Christ. He is the only true God, and he is eternal life.

[21] Dear children, keep away from anything that might take God's place in your hearts.

Whoever has the Son has life; whoever does not have God's Son does not have life.
The choice is yours.

In the words highlighted on the last page, John summarizes the choice facing everyone: If you want God's life for you, it's found in Jesus alone. By drawing circles in the ways we talked about on pages iv-vi, you can illustrate the essence of your life story: You are either inhabited by Jesus or not. You either have life or you don't.

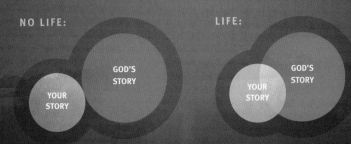

NO LIFE:

YOUR STORY

GOD'S STORY

LIFE:

YOUR STORY

GOD'S STORY

When my story can be totally explained without Jesus, I don't have him or the life he alone provides. But when my story can only be fully explained by including Jesus-in-me, I do have the life he alone provide

Q: What can you do to have Jesus in your life?

A: BELIEVE in Jesus!

Jesus replied, . . . Spend your energy seeking the eternal life that the Son of Man can give you. For God the Father has given me the seal of his approval."

They replied, "We want to perform God's works, too. What should we do?"

Jesus told them, "This is the only work God wants from you: Believe in the one he has sent." (John 6:26-29)

Shift who you BELIEVE in—who you trust—entirely away from your own rebellious (sinful) self. Put your trust completely in Jesus.

"Don't let your hearts be troubled. Trust in God, and trust also in me. . . . When everything is ready, I will come and get you, so that you will always be with me where I am. And you know the way to where I am going."

"No, we don't know, Lord," Thomas said. "We have no idea where you are going, so how can we know the way?"

Jesus told him, "I am the way, the truth, and the life. No one can come to the Father except through me." (John 14:1-6)

Jesus' death on the cross paid the price for your sins. BELIEVE it, and act on what you BELIEVE by asking God to forgive you, thanking him for his love and mercy.

He came into the very world he created, but the world didn't recognize him. He came to his own people, and even they rejected him. But to all who believed him and accepted him, he gave the right to become children of God. They are reborn—not with a physical birth resulting from human passion or plan, but a birth that comes from God. (John 1:10-13)

If we claim we have no sin, we are only fooling ourselves and not living in the truth. But if we confess our sins to him, he is faithful and just to forgive us our sins and to cleanse us from all wickedness. If we claim we have not sinned, we are calling God a liar and showing that his word has no place in our hearts.

My dear children, I am writing this to you so that you will not sin. But if anyone does sin, we have an advocate who pleads our case before the Father. He is Jesus Christ, the one who is truly righteous. He himself is the sacrifice that atones for our sins—and not only our sins but the sins of all the world. (1 John 1:8–2:2)

Jesus' resurrection proves he has the power to give you the brand-new life he taught about. BELIEVE it, and act on what you BELIEVE by learning what Jesus wants for your life, living in obedience to him, and making him known in your world. You will find yourself in great company—and the others around you who already know Jesus will be a great help in learning what life with Jesus looks like.

Eight days later the disciples were together again, and this time Thomas was with them. The doors were locked; but suddenly, as before, Jesus was standing among them. "Peace be with you," he said. Then he said to Thomas, "Put your finger here, and look at my hands. Put your hand into the wound in my side. Don't be faithless any longer. Believe!"

"My Lord and my God!" Thomas exclaimed.

Then Jesus told him, "You believe because you have seen me. Blessed are those who believe without seeing me."

The disciples saw Jesus do many other miraculous signs in addition to the ones recorded in this book. But these are written so that you may continue to believe that Jesus is the Messiah, the Son of God, and that by believing in him you will have life by the power of his name. (John 20:26-31)

All the believers devoted themselves to the apostles' teaching, and to fellowship, and to sharing in meals (including the Lord's Supper), and to prayer.

A deep sense of awe came over them all, and the apostles performed many miraculous signs and wonders. And all the believers met together in one place and shared everything they had. They sold their property and possessions and shared the money with those in need. They worshiped together at the Temple each day, met in homes for the Lord's Supper, and shared their meals with great joy and generosity—all the while praising God and enjoying the goodwill of all the people. And each day the Lord added to their fellowship those who were being saved. (Acts 2:42-47)

As you BELIEVE, Jesus will work miraculously within you to help you BECOME more and more like him. Watch how your life story, like those you read about in these pages, changes forever. Watch how God uses your new life story to change your friends.

Jesus replied, "I assure you, no one can enter the Kingdom of God without being born of water and the Spirit. Humans can reproduce only human life, but the Holy Spirit gives birth to spiritual life. So don't be surprised when I say, 'You must be born again.' The wind blows wherever it wants. Just as you can hear the wind but can't tell where it comes from or where it is going, so you can't explain how people are born of the Spirit." (John 3:5-8)

You say you have faith, for you believe that there is one God. Good for you! Even the demons believe this, and they tremble in terror. How foolish! Can't you see that faith without good deeds is useless?

Don't you remember that our ancestor Abraham was shown to be right with God by his actions when he offered his son Isaac on the altar? You see, his faith and his actions worked together. His actions made his faith complete. And so it happened just as the Scriptures say: "Abraham believed God, and God counted him as righteous because of his faith." He was even called the friend of God. So you see, we are shown to be right with God by what we do, not by faith alone. (James 2:19-23)